# Power,
# Public Opinion,
# and Policy
# in a Metropolitan
# Community

# H. George Frederickson
# Linda Schluter O'Leary

The Praeger Special Studies program—
utilizing the most modern and efficient book
production techniques and a selective
worldwide distribution network—makes
available to the academic, government, and
business communities significant, timely
research in U.S. and international economic, social, and political development.

# Power, Public Opinion, and Policy in a Metropolitan Community

A Case Study of Syracuse, New York

PRAEGER SPECIAL STUDIES IN U.S. ECONOMIC, SOCIAL, AND POLITICAL ISSUES

**Praeger Publishers**   New York   Washington   London

PRAEGER PUBLISHERS
111 Fourth Avenue, New York, N.Y. 10003, U.S.A.
5, Cromwell Place, London S.W.7, England

Published in the United States of America in 1973
by Praeger Publishers, Inc.

© 1973 by Praeger Publishers, Inc.

Library of Congress Catalog Card Number: 72-90665

Printed in the United States of America

For Mary and Michael

Urbanization is the challenge of our times. The concentration of people in huge cities has created crises in education, housing, transportation, poverty, law enforcement, health, and pollution. The governments that must meet these crises are being tested as never before—tested in their political leadership, in their fiscal capacity, in their administrative abilities, and in their humanity. This book is about political power, public opinion, and the policy-making process in an urban area being tested by such crises.

The study took three years. Many people helped. Joseph Ohren and Howard Magnas were our graduate assistants, and Sylvia Paine provided editorial assistance. Laura Spaulding typed the manuscript. Steven Brams and Michael K. O'Leary gave methodological and editorial guidance. The citizens of our community and their leaders provided time for our opinion polling and interviewing. The Syracuse University Computing Center supported our work. The warm and hospitable environment provided by the staff of our home base, the Metropolitan Studies Program of the Maxwell Graduate School of Citizenship and Public Affairs of Syracuse University, greatly facilitated our work. And, most important, the research could not have been conducted were it not for the generous support of the Allied Chemical Corporation.

We will share credit in equal measure. For errors of substance, method, or interpretation, each will blame the other.

Syracuse, New York
February 1971

68684

## LIST OF TABLES AND FIGURES

## LIST OF FIGURES

The community power study asks who within the community has power. It generally neglects to ask how much power exists within the community and to what extent the exercise of this power is related to the demands of the rank and file. We do not know how much power the community official wields as compared to the power of those outside the community who are able to influence its affairs nor do we have information about the fit between public opinion within the community on a wide variety of issues and the activities of public officials in regard to these issue areas. In attempting to respond to these gaps in our knowledge we have done a new community power study in Syracuse, New York the center of a Standard Metropolitan Statistical Area (SMSA) considered to be coextensive with Onondaga County.

We built our study on those two most illustrious predecessors, Roscoe C. Martin's Decisions in Syracuse and Linton C. Freeman's Syracuse study, Patterns of Local Community Leadership.[1] Martin and Munger's conclusions have much in common with Robert A. Dahl's New Haven findings. They found that there had been a shift from a monolithic to a pluralistic power structure. When a range of decisions is considered, different groups hold power in different areas. Freeman's study seconded this conclusion. According to Freeman leadership in Syracuse is spread among a multiplicity of groups. Both studies, as we discuss in greater detail below, indicated that power in Syracuse is dispersed. The individual or institution involved in any issue is dependent upon the substantive area of the issue. Our study accepted these findings as premises. We hope that we have developed further the implications and shed light on questions that were raised by these studies.

The first phase of our study, done in the summer of 1967, was directed to an empirical analysis of the role played by public opinion in the policy-making process. Our concern was the opinions of citizens as to the ordering of priorities in the metropolitan area. The second phase of our study, begun in 1969, was focused on patterns of power among local influentials on the one hand and between local influentials and state and federal elites on the other. We concentrated our research on four critical community functions—law enforcement, social services, education, and water pollution control. By interviewing the officials themselves and with the aid of a less obtrusive corroborative technique, we made a determination of the extent to which decisions relevant to these four community-based functional activities are made at the local, state, and federal levels of government.

Our rationale for a new study of Syracuse was twofold. We believe that a study of the influence wielded by locals done within the framework developed for community power studies is a valuable addition to that body of literature concerned with the federal system in relation to local governments. Many sociologists and political scientists believe that, short of the nation itself, communities are obsolete. Scott Greer, for example, has said,

> The process of increase in [societal] scale, nurtured in cities and once thought of as unique to them, will have so transformed the society as to eliminate the need for cities. . . . Among the casualties may also be the concept of local government as a democratic policy.[2]

Others, such as Roscoe Martin, conclude that the federal system has been invigorated by the addition of a third metropolitan partner and that the federal system has evolved from a two- to a three-part system, with the federal government frequently interacting directly with local governments.[3]

Knowledge of the nature of the U.S. federal system as it affects one particular community was not our sole rationale for embarking upon a new community study. To be more esoteric but perhaps more significant, we were concerned with the larger question of whether individuals do exercise any control over the public decisions that affect them.

The United States is the most pronounced example of "mass society" known to man. The concept of democracy, however, has not been conceived as an effective tool for mass governance. This is clear from the most cursory study of Western democratic thought. U.S. political thinkers do not provide an exception to the belief that "democracy" is basically a grass-roots system of governance with authority emanating from the people and decisions implemented in their name. Throughout the course of U.S. political history our foremost democratic thinkers have insisted that the United States be small and its government limited. Twentieth-century philosophers of democracy have been forced to accept the size, the scale, and the complexity of the modern United States. John Dewey, for example, was the first philosopher of democracy to accept the fact that the United States is big, industrial, and urban and is destined to become more, not less, so. He saw the problem of mass democracy as one of creating conditions under which a disjoint, dispersed "inchoate public" could function democratically. He believed that a democratic sociopolitical system consisted of individuals having a responsible share of power according to their capacity in forming and directing the activities of the groups to which they belong and in participating according to need in the values that the groups sustain.[4]

Contemporary political theorists share Dewey's concern for participatory democracy, for the existence of real freedom, and for the creation of publics. The question of whether democracy can and/or does exist in the United States today is asked by the new radical as well as by the suburban parents he left behind. An example of the radical's concern is the historically significant Port Huron Statement of Students for a Democratic Society (SDS). Written by "people of this generation, bred in at least modest comfort, housed in universities, looking uncomfortably to the world we inherit," it is dedicated to "the search for truly democratic alternatives to the present and a commitment to social experimentation with them, [as] a worthy and fulfilling human enterprise." It insists that most Americans are in withdrawal from public life and thus from any collective effort at directing their own affairs. It affirms the value of "wrenching" control of government from the elite and creating publics to take an active part in guiding the affairs of the country.[5]

That the control of government is in the hands of an elite is not as certain as the radicals would have us believe. Still, there are many who feel powerless in guiding their own affairs. Their numbers are not restricted to the minority of Americans who are obviously excluded because of their race, poverty, or incapacity. Robert C. Wood, in Suburbia: Its People and Their Politics, suggests that the suburban impulse toward grass-roots government is a function of the belief that local government needs to be reclaimed.[6] In evaluating the proliferation of suburban governments that are quite content to maintain their autonomy despite wastefulness and inefficiency of many governmental units with overlapping jurisdictions and the concomitant duplication of some services and lack of availability of others because the units are too small to provide them, one concludes that the benefits of consolidation do not tempt many to give up the feeling of control that comes with participating in a small government unit.

One certainly cannot say that the only problem besetting the metropolis is a belief in alienation from the sources of power and decision-making. Still, the conventional wisdom tells us that the urban dweller, the citizen of the metropolis, believes himself to be particularly dispossessed. For one thing the metropolitan area is too large and the services it provides are too complex to be kept in check by the populace. Furthermore, local government officials themselves are believed to be powerless in the face of ever-expanding state and federal governments.

It is within this context that we developed and investigated our hypotheses about public opinion in Syracuse in relation to policy-making and the role of the local official in making decisions relevant to his community. We began with the assumption that knowledge of public priorities can be gained by the use of general survey techniques.

After taking a stratified random sample of the population of Syracuse, an open selection technique was used to assess each respondent's set of urban priority preferences. When all 1,036 persons in the sample were taken together, we found education, police protection, and water pollution control to be the first- , second-, and third-level priorities. In disaggregating urban priorities on the basis of respondent's residence, we found a clear urban-suburban contrast on the basis of residence. While city and suburban residents agreed that education and law enforcement were the two most compelling priorities, the city residents considered direct such human needs as employment, housing, and welfare next, while suburbanites consider water adequacy and pollution more important. We found similar differences when we disaggregated our data on the basis of education and income differences within the sample of respondents.

We then made an attempt to assess the actual or real priorities of the collective governments of Onondaga County by means of an analysis of their pattern of expenditures. On the basis of this comparison we found that public priorities attached to education are being met by the proportion of total spending devoted to that function. Central city residents—persons with lower education and lower incomes—are receiving moderate preferences in the welfare and housing spending categories. Conversely, suburbanites and higher income and education publics are not receiving their preferences for water pollution abatement programs as directly. All groups, but especially central city and lower income and education persons, indicate strong priorities for law enforcement spending, yet spending for this function does not appear to match the demand indicated. Still, we must conclude that there is a remarkably close fit between urban priorities as delineated by the metropolitan constituency and the actual foci of local government activity in Syracuse.

Once we were satisfied that we had a well-developed knowledge of public opinion and priorities, we used that knowledge as the backdrop or context for a study of local government itself. We chose four functional areas of local endeavor for detailed examination: education, social welfare, law enforcement and water pollution abatement. These areas of public activity are considered to be the most significant by the citizens of Syracuse. In addition they account for the major share of public spending. We carried the question of local control over local functions further by making a determination of the extent to which local government officials exercise significant influence when compared to their state and federal counterparts. There were two aspects to this phase of our study. We wanted to know whether locals exercised influence vis-a-vis state and federal officials generally; we also wanted specific information on decision-making relevant to the determination of the structure as well as the day-to-day operations of the institutions that embody these governmental functions.

Our most significant conclusion was probably that of variance from one institution to the next. Of the four groups of officials—educators, social welfare administrators, law enforcers, and water control officials—the educators are the most autonomous with respect to state and federal inputs to the decision-making process. Water pollution abatement in Onondaga County is, as one might expect, most influenced by higher level decision-makers. The generalization we were able to make on the basis of all four functional areas taken together was that of locals sharing power with state and federal officials on a quite equal basis. In other words students of power in the community must recognize the fact of a vertical dimension to community power, but at the same time our evidence does not support the argument that locals are powerless and that local government is obsolete.

Our findings, then, indicate that the people in the community we studied substantially approve of the priorities for governmental expenditure existent within that community. Furthermore, local government officials, their closest representative spokesmen, do exercise a significant share of influence in carrying out the business of the locality. Our findings are presented in three parts. In Part One we offer our conclusions about power in Syracuse. Part Two develops the tie between power and public opinion. In Part Three we detail the policy-making implications of our research.

# COMMUNITY POWER
# IN SYRACUSE

## APPROACHES TO COMMUNITY POWER

Ever since Plato's <u>Republic</u> scholars have concerned themselves
with men's relations with one another within the community context.
Modern systematic analysis of the community, its nature, and the
relations among men within it dates back only a few decades, however.
Earlier the community was examined as a whole, the researchers
immersing themselves within the local community for long periods
of time, with change in the community as the object of investigation.
A classic study of this type conducted during the depression revealed
the impact of local business on the economy and the effect of a national
firm's gaining predominance in one community's economy.[1] Only
gradually did scholars isolate specific aspects of the community for
intensive investigation—for example, the distribution of prestige in
W. Lloyd Warner and S. Lunt's case study of Yankee City.[2]

During the 1950s, however, power and decision-making in the
community became the focus of attention among scholars, especially
political scientists and sociologists. The impetus behind these new
efforts was the publication in 1953 of a study of Atlanta, Georgia,
which seriously challenged the assumption of a one-to-one correspondence between office-holding and authoritative decision-making at the
local level of government.[3] The Atlanta study suggested that while
institutions and formal associations are significant in the execution
of policy, policy determination often takes place outside these formal
groupings; in the case of Atlanta it is dominated by a small number
of business leaders who constitute a covert economic elite.

The importance of Hunter's work lies not so much in the results
of his study—in the pattern of influence he identified—but rather in the
methodology he employed, utilizing sociometry to demonstrate

4 POWER, PUBLIC OPINION, AND POLICY

interpersonal behavior patterns related to community influence.[4]
Hunter, though not the first to use the method, developed and improved
what has come to be called the reputational technique for assessing
community power. A selected group of informants was asked to identify
the top leaders or influentials in the community; then the relationships
among these individuals were ascertained. It was only after Hunter
that communities were studied solely for purposes of testing or refuting
hypotheses about community power and decision-making.[5]

The question of the nature of the relationship between office-
holders and decision-making pursued in the Atlanta study has not yet
definitively been answered. Some of the large number of research
efforts stimulated by these findings support Hunter's conclusion,
whereas others dispute his interpretation of a covert ruling economic
elite. Not only Hunter's results but also his methodology and implied
assumptions came to be challenged in a debate that has yet to end.
Critics alleged that Hunter began with the unwarranted assumption
that a top group did rule the community, as indicated by his question,
"Who are the 'top leaders' in the community?" Many political scientists thought it more useful to ask the question of who shares in
ruling. Rather than seeking to determine which individuals in the
community had a reputation for being influential, they regarded reputation as irrelevant or secondary and focused on concrete manifestations of influence in the process of decision-making.

Hunter and his conclusions and methodology stand at one extreme
in the debate. His concerns and, until recently, the reputational
technique or some variation of it are shared by researchers, generally
sociologists, who are interested in the exercise of power in social,
religious, economic, and political institutions. Hunter discerned a
monolithic community power structure consisting of about 40 business
leaders, all of whom knew one another and belonged to one of five
cliques. Informally, this group determined the policy to be carried out
by public officials and association officers.

At the other extreme are those scholars who assert that administrators and politicians are the decision-makers and are influenced
by the electorate. These researchers question the existence of a
single center of power or of a cohesive coalition of groups wielding
power. They generally conclude that the distribution of power is
dispersed among multiple centers, none completely sovereign nor
overlapping or coalescing in any consistent way, and that class lines
are not the determinants of that distribution. Robert Dahl's Who
Governs? was a seminal attempt to develop an alternative to the
elitists' research methodologies.[6] By focusing on participation in
political decision-making in New Haven, identifying the persons who
actually took part in concrete decisions and whose suggestions were
actually followed, Dahl made a comprehensive effort to develop an
empirically based theory of democratic pluralism.

## COMMUNITY POWER IN SYRACUSE

Roscoe Martin, Frank Munger, and their associates studied community power in Syracuse, using a decision-making approach.  Their
conclusions about the evolution of the power structure have much in
common with Dahl's New Haven findings.  After analyzing 22 cases of
decision-making in the Syracuse metropolitan area, Martin and Munger
concluded that there has been a shift from a monolithic power structure
to a pluralistic structure.  They found that when a range of decisions
is considered different groups seem to hold power in different areas.
Among the groups involved there was a low level of participation in
the making of decisions.  Furthermore, no group tested its strength
in a majority of decisions, and most groups were involved in only a
few.[7]  They concluded that

> there tend to be as many decision centers as there are
> important decision areas, which means that the decision-
> making power is fragmented among the institutions, agen-
> cies, and individuals which cluster about these areas. . . .
> In reality there appear to be many kinds of community
> power, with one kind differing from another in so many
> fundamental ways as to make virtually impossible a
> meaningful comparison.

Thus, their findings eliminate an interpretation of a monolithic
power structure in Syracuse.  Linton Freeman's study of decision-
making in Syracuse seconds this conclusion.[8]  According to Freeman,
leadership in Syracuse is spread among a multiplicity of groups.  The
fact that "issue clusters" are predominantly content oriented indicates
that interests are highly specialized and that most decision-makers
are either amateur or professional experts.  In education decisions
education administrators, the Parent Teacher Association (PTA), and
the school boards are highly influential.  These groups are not influential in law enforcement or welfare decisions.  In these substantive
specialties the logical specialists, officials, and interest groups are
influential; thus there are plural centers of power.
There is much congruity between the Martin and Munger study
and the Freeman study.  Both agree that power in Syracuse is dispersed.
Which individual or institution is involved in any issue depends upon
the substantive character of the issue.  It might therefore be profitable
to use the reputational technique to isolate decision-makers in a
sampling of policy areas without assuming the existence of a coterie
of undercover leaders from whom authority ultimately must come.
Both the Martin and Munger study and the Freeman study suggest

that the professionals involved in issue areas either themselves make
the decisions relevant to their functions or know who does make them.
In fact Martin and Munger say that

> interviews in which power is attributed have typically been
> with . . . business leaders, rather than with the government
> officials on whom power must finally be exerted if it is to
> affect government action. . . . We have few equivalents on
> the municipal level of the state legislative studies of Oliver
> Garceau, Corinne Silverman, and others, in which state
> legislators have been asked to express their own opinions
> as to the relative importance of the interest groups that
> purport to wield power; lacking such studies, we have little
> evidence as to the perceptions of community power of the
> governmental officials themselves.[9]

## THE CONCEPT OF COMMUNITY

The local community, as is evident from the above, has been
examined from a variety of perspectives. Some have seen it as a
convenient laboratory for testing general propositions concerning
political power, leadership, or the decision-making process generically. The local laboratory is popular because it is ordinarily easier
to secure interview time with a metropolitan influential than with a
prime minister. Others have been interested in local political structures as examples of the effect of social stratification. Whatever the
approach, it seems that a significant topic—extracommunity decisions
affecting policy within the community—has been overlooked by most
students of the community.

Recently, scholars of the community have recognized that the
traditional way of viewing the community as a unit is inadequate.
Institutions and groups within the community have been isolated and
studied with little concern for the social, political, and economic
context in which the community rests. Roland Warren concludes, "The
relatively differentiated parts which constitute the contemporary
American community are related increasingly to the outside world
not so much as parts of the local community but as parts of specialized
extra-community systems to which they belong."[10]

The older concepts of community are inadequate because geographic locale of residents no longer coincides with the area upon
which they are dependent for fulfillment of their needs. Rather than
being characterized as an entity in itself with discernible limits, the
community can be defined more realistically, and more usefully, in
theoretical terms, as a social system.

The social system concept is based on the idea of structured interaction between two or more units, either persons or groups. The process of interaction among units is basic, but not all instances of interaction identified by the investigator are equally important. Warren borrows from Talcott Parsons in describing a social system:

> A plurality of individual actors interacting with each other
> in a situation which has at least a physical or environ-
> mental aspect, actors who are motivated in terms of a
> tendency to the 'optimization of gratification' and whose
> relation to their situations, including each other, is defined
> and mediated in terms of a system of culturally structured
> and shared symbols.[11]

All social systems have four coordinates: goal attainment, or the gratification of the units of the system; adaptation, or the manipulation of the environment in the interests of goal attainment; integration, or the attachment of member units to each other; and tension, or the malintegration of units seen as systems in themselves.

Warren, then, describes a community as a system of systems. "A community, even a small one, includes a great many different institutions and organizations and the formal and informal subgroups that grow up within them. These organizations and groups are social systems and they are part of the social system of the community."[12] In other words community as system is made up of different levels of system and subsystem, such as the municipal government, the East Side Baptist Church, the branch plant of ABC Products Corporation, and the American Red Cross Chapter. Many of these are integral parts of larger social systems—the Southern Baptist Convention, the national company, the American National Red Cross—that extend far beyond the confines of the community. The community as a social system does not, however, similarly relate in any such direct, systematic way to any larger system. The relationship of the community as such to a larger social system is by means of the relation of its constituent subsystems to their extracommunity systems. In this view the community is not a static, discernible entity but a congeries of moving subsystems that interact with each other and with extracommunity referents.

Warren provides a useful conceptual tool in his study of the community by using the idea of horizontal and vertical ties to distinguish between patterns of interaction among units within the community and between community units and their extracommunity systems. Despite the fact that, as has been indicated, the vertical pattern assumes greater significance in the contemporary community, that pattern has been all but ignored by students of community power.

Typically, after only the briefest references to the increasing involvement between the local community and extracommunity units, such
as the state and federal governments, regional and national economic
concerns, and communications media, the researcher then goes on to
concern himself with who makes decisions in the community.

A recent commentator on community power studies reaffirms
this oversight in referring to the studies of Robert Presthus and Linton
Freeman:

> In both cases, some of the major decisions affecting the
> communities are made outside the communities—by the
> state and federal governments mainly, by nationally based
> corporations and trade unions in some cases—although
> this fact is most often ignored by the investigators of local
> community power structure.[13]

Presthus, in Men at the Top, devotes consideration to what he
calls the external bases of community power. He concludes that political leaders in both Edgewood and Riverview, and especially in Riverview, relied upon connections with politicians at the state and federal
level for the major resources that solidified their power at the local
level. While these connections brought both communities financial
aid for health, education, housing, and flood control, they also seriously
lessened their autonomy. In return for state and federal funding, as
well as for economic aid from private sources, local governments
were obliged to meet various standards and conditions imposed from
the outside. Thus, the initiation and control of local decisions was
shared, to a considerable extent, with external sources of power.[14]

Freeman, on the other hand, mentions decisions made outside
the community only to exclude them in establishing criteria for the
selection of issues to be studied.[15] This approach, as Rose suggests,
is more common to the study of community decision-making. In fact
a careful investigation of the literature has uncovered only one
empirical analysis of the significance of extracommunity sources of
power. John Walton develops a theoretical explanation of how power
is distributed in local communities.[16] He hypothesizes a relationship
between various power distributions and different forms of community
action. As communities become increasingly interdependent with
extracommunity institutions, changes in the local normative order
ensue, producing more competitive power arrangements.

By perusal of the community power literature Walton obtained
a complete list of studies, which he defined as a universe. The studies
were coded in terms of a number of variables, such as region, population, size, industrialization, and economic diversity. In addition he
also coded the type of power structure identified in each study by use

of four categories: (a) Pyramidal—a monolithic, monopolistic, or single cohesive leadership group; (b) Factional—at least two durable factions that compete for advantages; (c) Coalitional—leadership varies with issues and is made up of fluid coalitions of interested persons and groups; (d) Amorphous—no persistent pattern of leadership or power exercised on the local level.

Walton then sought evidence of association or lack of association between these two sets of variables.[17] He observed a relationship among competitive power structure and the presence of absentee-owned corporations, competitive party politics, adequate economic resources, and satellite status.[18] A large number of variables, including region, population size, population composition, industrialization, economic diversity, and type of local government, were not found to be related to type of power structure. In attempting to explain these observations, Walton suggests that normative expectations (consensus or conflict of values and goals among the residents of the community) bear a relationship to the power structure. Conflict within the community can be taken as an indicator of that relationship. In addition to the positive relationship noted, in those communities where change was observed (longitudinal studies) the trend was toward a greater vertical dispersion of power.

Thus, each of the variables associated with competitive power structure reflects the interdependence of community and extracommunity centers of power. As an example, Walton suggests that a high proportion of absentee-owned industry indicates that many community-relevant decisions are controlled by the personnel and interests of national corporate bodies whose influence may stem either from a deliberate intervention in local affairs or from aloofness to local responsibility.[19] In a similar fashion competitive political parties often reflect the involvement of county, state, and national party organizations in a struggle for control of local constituencies.[20]

The mechanism by which interdependence, or increasing relevance of what Walton calls the vertical axis of community organization, affects the distribution of community power is the disruption of the local normative order associated with the existing power structure. Development along the vertical axis involves the introduction of new interests and new institutional relationships, which have the effect of disrupting consensual normative relationships through differentiation of allegiances on the part of community members, as well as through the introduction of new resources and sanctions into the community. Local organizations with vertical ties to extracommunity institutions frequently share in the capital and human resources of the extracommunity institution. Walton gives the example of an absentee-owned corporation gaining importance as a local tax contributor, employer, and supplier as a result of receiving funds and skilled personnel from an expansion of the local operation. Such resources carry with them potential sanctions. In Walton's example some of these sanctions include the threat to locate elsewhere, the threat of cutbacks or other actions having an adverse effect on the local economy, and support or nonsupport of local political candidates or issues.

Development along the vertical axis has the effect, then, of disrupting consensual normative expectations by the introduction of new interests and new institutional relationships into the community. The greater the number of community organizations with vertical ties, the more frequent and the more inclusive the contests surrounding the decision-making process.[21] Walton concludes by presenting six hypotheses wherein variables that reflect the interdependence of the community and the larger society, such as absentee ownership, party competition, adequate economic resources, and satellite status, are associated with competitive power structures, whereas those variables that reflect only intercommunity changes, such as economic diversity and population increase, are not so associated.[22] The thrust of his study is a recognition of the necessity of locating the source of community change in the relationships between community and extracommunity institutions. The appropriate unit of analysis is not the community itself, as most students of local power have assumed, but rather the relationship between the community and the institutions of the larger society.


## THE CONCEPT OF POWER

In moving toward a broadened examination of community power in Syracuse, it is necessary to pause for a moment to discuss the concept of power, its application and meaning in the past, and the present perspective.[23] Failure to fully define or describe power adequately is considered a fundamental weakness in the contemporary study of community power. The confusion surrounding the concept of power is in part the result of lack of care in distinguishing among several closely related concepts. Power, influence, control, authority, and leadership are frequently used interchangeably, often on the pretext that they are synonymous in popular usage.

The problem of defining power presents another difficulty. Power analysts agree that, at a minimum, power is involved when one person or group achieves compliance from others in respect to the distribution of a given value. Beyond this level, however, other variables become involved. For instance power may be associated with the threat or use of sanctions, both positive and negative. The relationship among individuals is said to entail power when one actor is able to induce other actors to behave in a way they would not behave otherwise. That is, the power of actor A over actor B is observed by noting the difference between the way B actually behaves and the way he would behave if A were not present.

Authority and influence are often viewed as subclasses of power. Whereas authority is an official capacity maintained by one in a formal hierarchical structure in order to achieve compliance, influence is an unofficial quality held by one who may lack formal authority but is nevertheless able to induce others to obey him. Both are considered necessary to the effective wielding of power, although the operation of either, the resources used, and the results achieved may be entirely different.

The concept of power may also be distinguished as actual or potential realization of will. If power is defined as potential, then in the confrontation between opposing forces the fact that the ultimate result can be described as a victory does not necessarily mean that only one of the parties had power; there may have been power on both sides, but the potential of one side may have been greater than that of the other. Power as a potential for control and power as the exercise of control itself are not mutually exclusive; persons who exercise power must have had a power potential, but not all persons who hold potential power do in fact exercise power.

Power is also seen as inherent in institutions rather than in people, a view that emphasizes the position of institutional bases of power. It may also be viewed as the result of specific interpersonal relationships, with the consequent focus upon the qualities of the power holder.[24] Further views on power may result from exploring such aspects as the means to secure compliance; the resources, base, scope, and extent of power; and the consequences for both sides of the use of power.

The debate as to how power may best be defined is meaningful in that the way it is studied is closely related to the way it is defined. Karl Deutsch's concept of power best lends itself to operationalization in the context of this study. According to Deutsch, it is in connection with will and character that the power of a system, person, or organization must be understood. Character is the more or less stable inner program of a system, person, or organization. Power is the extent to which character can be exercised. Thus, whereas character is the structure of habits and memories acquired in the past, power is the ability to impose extrapolations or projections of this inner structure on the environment. Deutsch distinguishes these qualities as gross power from net power, or the difference between the probability of change imposed on the outside world and the probability of critical or relevant change occurring in the inner structure of the individual or organization.[25]

Deutsch uses Talcott Parsons' systems theory in operationalizing power. As described earlier, Parsons distinguishes four functional prerequisites for any social system: maintenance, adaptation, goal attainment, and integration. Each of these four main functions is served by all subsystems of the society, but to each of them there corresponds a major subsystem. Among four main functional subsystems there are six possible flows of interchange connecting each of the four main subsystems with each of the three others. These flows of interchange are schematized in Figure 1.

The flows of interchange are either barter-type transactions (i.e., households delivering labor to the economy and eventually receiving consumer goods from it) or, in more advanced systems, social mechanisms that are "narrowly specialized in generality."[26] Deutsch calls such mechanisms "currencies." For example cash is the currency in the exchange of labor for goods. Household members exchange their labor for money wages, and these wages are turned into consumer spending; for the consumer expenditures goods are obtained. There are, then, two transaction flows in each direction: One is specialized in terms of the physical things and acts concerned; the other is generalized and flexible in terms of currency employed.

Power is the most important currency in interchanges between political systems and other subsystems, but it is not the sole currency. The political system depends to a large extent on what Deutsch calls the "fabric of coordinated expectations." Governments can promise to back with sanctions many more of their binding decisions, rules,

FIGURE 1

Flows of Interchange

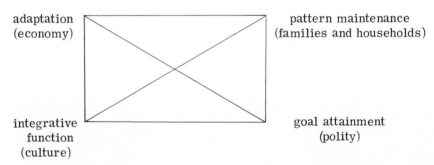

adaptation
(economy)

pattern maintenance
(families and households)

integrative
function
(culture)

goal attainment
(polity)

Source: Karl W. Deutsch, The Nerves of Government (New York: The Free Press, 1963), pp. 116-17.

and laws, and to do so against many more people than nongovernmental
institutions. Although the coordination of human efforts toward the
attainment of goals may be facilitated by the use of power, for the
most part it is the coordination of habits that keeps things going.

> Power is thus neither the center nor the essence of
> politics. It is one of the currencies of politics, one of the
> important mechanisms of acceleration or of damage
> control where influence, habit, or voluntary coordination
> may have failed, or where these may have failed to serve
> adequately the function of goal attainment.[27]

Deutsch's analysis of power and of other currencies of political
interchange provides a fruitful approach to a study of decision-making.
It is simple. Direct assessments of potential for power or of power
itself can be circumvented in favor of examination of those currencies,
such as communication flow, that are readily accessible. Enough
agreement exists within the power literature to conclude that the term
power might profitably be avoided—that isolation of proxies of power
will yield data relevant to the purposes here in studying the decision-
making process. Even Deutsch's definition of power (the imposition
of a system's character on its environment less the amount of change
in the system imposed by this confrontation with the environment),
although possible to operationalize, perhaps through psychoanalytic
techniques, would be difficult to apply, to say the least. And, as is
obvious from the above discussion of the previous analysis of power,
a great deal of semantic confusion can be avoided by calling the
behavioral variables isolated proxies of power.

## A NEW CONCEPT OF COMMUNITY POWER

As has been seen, the community power study asks: "Who has
power within the community?" Community power studies generally
neglect to ask how much power exists within the community. Recent
research efforts allow one to predict the probable loci of power in
the community, yet one does not know how much power the local
influential exercises as compared to the power of those outside the
community who are able to influence community affairs. The emphasis
in this study is on the patterns of influence among local influentials
on the one hand and between local influentials and state and federal
elites on the other.

Morton Grodzins has made a strong case for the influence of
local political and governmental units in the national political process:

> The correct conclusion to be drawn from consideration of
> local influence on federal and state programs is not that
> the local view is controlling. It is rather that the localities
> are full and powerful participants in the process of decision-
> making . . . They are not always and everywhere decisive,
> but in most programs at most times some groups of locali-
> ties (or, a single one) exercises a substantial influence.[28]

The research reported in the following pages is designed to shed light
on the question of local leaders' power and the relationship of local
power to power at higher levels of government.

Here, community is being conceptualized as a number of systems
and subsystems with extracommunity referents. Examination is
focused upon the flow of interchange, in Deutsch's terminology, between community-based systems and their extracommunity ties. The
purpose is to discern the proportion of decision-making made on the
horizontal axis of the community as opposed to the proportion made
on the vertical axis for each of four subsystems of the community
studied: social services, education, police, and pollution control. The
entire spectrum of each institution's activity has been studied for a
given period of time rather than a number of decisions made at different
times. The approach is process oriented. Epic decisions, the direct,
sensational confrontations within the sphere of any system's activity,
may be the most significant acts of that institution's operation, and
an approach in which the process of interaction is examined over time
makes it possible to generalize about influence relationships.

Further rationale for a process approach to the study of influence
may be found in a most significant theoretical discussion of power,
Peter Bachrach and Norton Baratz's "Two Faces of Power."[29] Only
one face of power is manifest in the outcome of the overt decision-
making processes. The other consists of the capacity of individuals
and groups to prevent threatening issues or contests from arising.
In criticizing the approach wherein "crucial issues" are selected for
investigation, the authors point out two fundamental defects. First,
the approach takes no account of the fact that power may be, and often
is, exercised by confining the scope of decision-making to "safe"
issues. Second, it provides no objective criteria for distinguishing
between "important" and "unimportant" issues arising in the political
arena. In illustrating the first, Bachrach and Baratz explain:

> Of course power is exercised when A participates in the
> making of decisions that affect B. But power is also
> exercised when A devotes his energies to creating or
> reinforcing social and political values and institutional
> practices that limit the scope of the political process to

public consideration of only those issues which are comparatively innocuous to A.[30]

Bachrach and Baratz insist that the researcher begin not by
asking, "Who rules?" as does the sociologist or "Does anyone have
power?" as does the pluralist but by investigating the particular
"mobilization of bias"[31]—the dominant values, the myths, and the
established political procedures and rules of the game—in the institution being examined. From an investigation of this sort the researcher
can discover which persons or groups gain from the existing bias and
which are handicapped by it. Next, the researcher should investigate
the dynamics of non-decision-making—the extent to which the establishment is able to limit the scope of actual decision-making to "safe"
issues. The conceptualization and operationalization of the decision-
making process in this book meets these dicta in that the plan is to
study the day-to-day life of institutions rather than certain so-called
crucial decisions.

## METHODOLOGY

The community has been defined as a social system identified
by structured interaction between two or more units, either persons
or groups. It has been suggested that each system has a more or less
stable inner program that can be termed character and that the power
of the system can be viewed as the extent to which the system can act
out its character. The flow of interchange between community-based
subsystems, such as law enforcement, social services, education,
and water pollution control, and their extracommunity ties will be the
objects of investigation; an attempt will be made to determine the
extent to which decisions relevant to these community policy areas
are made at the local, state, and federal levels of government. The
following pages indicate some of the variables that will be used and
the authors' hypotheses.

### Community

As noted above, the combination of systems and units performing
the major functions that have locality relevance is the theoretical
definition of community.[32] By locality relevance is meant pertinence
to provision of goods or services to the population of a specific area.
This concept shall be operationalized by considering it to be those
systems that perform locality-relevant functions and that are located
within the Syracuse metropolitan area. The Syracuse metropolitan

area is usually considered coextensive with Onondaga County. Martin and Munger will be followed in accepting this view as the geographic operationalization of the concept here.[33]

## Locality-Relevant Functions

In operational terms locality-relevant functions are as follows:

Production-distribution-consumption concerns operations concerning those goods and services that are a part of daily living and access to which is desirable in the immediate locality. The economy is the most important social unit fulfilling this function.

Socialization is the process by which society transmits prevailing knowledge, social values, and behavior patterns to its individual members. Families and schools are those institutions most involved in this process.

Social control is the process through which a group influences the behavior of its members toward conformity with its norms. Included are formal government, police, and courts, as well as many other social units such as the family, the school, the church, and the social agency.

Social participation is action through religious organizations and voluntary associations.

Mutual support involves activities, such as care in time of sickness, the exchange of labor, or the helping out of a local family in time of economic distress, which traditionally have been performed by the primary group. Today, public welfare departments, private health and welfare agencies, governmental and commercial insurance companies, and many other units also fulfill such functions.

It is not the intention here to take account of every community system or subsystem having locality-relevant functions. Studies have been made previously of the change in power structure precipitated by the change from locally owned to national economic units.[34] Examination of the role played by family, friendship, and kinship groups is excluded by the nature of this study. The courts are also a special case outside the purview of the study in that historically and by constitutional dictate they are hierarchically organized with the locus of final authority at the apex. In the interests of time and efficiency voluntary associations are also excluded. They might, however, profitably be the focus of a future study. Only those governmental units that partially encompass the socialization, social control, social participation, and mutual support functions and that may be the most significant institutions fulfilling these functions shall be examined. The units involved are the Syracuse School District, the Onondaga County Department of Social Services, the Syracuse Police Department, the Onondaga County Sheriff's Department, and the Onondaga County Department of Public Works.[35]


## Power and Influence

A number of respondents were selected and each was asked to name those people on the local, state, and federal levels of government with whom they are in frequent communication and with whom they consider themselves to be in an influence relationship. They were further asked if they perceived the influence relationship to be symmetrical or asymmetrical and, if asymmetrical, in what direction. It was explained to the interviewee that by influence was meant ability to persuade the other of a point of view or an approach outside the realm of legal authority.


## Determination of Respondents

Several approaches were used to determine who is most significant in the making of decisions relevant to the community. Because the study is concerned with decision-making within given subsystems, the positional approach was used. The assumption that the administrative leaders of the subsystem in question will know who makes the decisions relating to the operation of that subsystem has the merits of simplicity and of common sense. If they who carry out orders do not know whence these orders come, who does?


## An Unobtrusive Measure

The interview technique is, in Eugene Webb and his associates' terms, an "obtrusive measure."[36] All kinds of confounding variables are introduced in the assessment of currency flow by the intrusion of the personality of the interviewee in response to the presence of an interviewer. Because the interviewee's behavior might be influenced by his perception of the expectations of the interviewer or by his wish to influence the interviewer in a certain way or to convince the interviewer of something, his responses within the context of the interview must be evaluated with the assumption that any of these possibilities may exist. For example, a local government official may need to exaggerate his own importance as opposed to the importance of officials at the state level of government. This need might arise from his own personality, from what he perceives to be the demands of his public, or from any one of a number of other reasons.

Therefore an additional measure of currency flow was used that is independent of the possibility of confusion by variables of this sort. By use of the interviewee's appointment calendar his departmental, nongovernmental community, local government, state government, and federal government contacts for a given period of time were tallied. It is realized that this measure is not strong enough to stand by itself; it is used only as an unobtrusive check on the primary method of gaining insight into the problem posed by the study.

# 2

**MEASURING
COMMUNITY
RELATIONS**

## INFLUENCE

Influence is a fundamental concept in social science, but, as indicated in Chapter 1, its widespread use as a term has not led scholars to be particularly clear or precise about its meaning. Without extensively reviewing the rather chaotic assortment of literature on influence, it was indicated that most studies have taken either of two basic approaches to the subject—one can be called the "power inventory" approach and the other the "behavioral" approach. The power inventory approach attempts to infer one actor's influence by taking note of the resources he possesses or to which he has access. This approach may nominally acknowledge the relational nature of influence but tends to concentrate on each individual's capabilities. The second approach attempts to estimate how one actor is able to change the behavior of another actor. The more that one is able to do so, the more influence he possesses. By way of a brief critique it is suggested that, whereas the techniques of the first approach are quite straightforward, the explanatory and even descriptive results are generally simplistic. The second approach, while potentially much more valuable, has not yet developed adequate techniques to fulfill the promise of the concepts.

The research in this part of the study is related to these two approaches, although it does not completely follow either of them. Actors' perceptions of their influence relations with others has been taken as one of the measures. At the very least perceptions constitute a relational property of influence and may occasionally serve as a resource that some actors can exploit to their own advantage. In this study the relative importance of perceptions for either the resource or the relational approach to influence is not, of course, established. An attempt has been made here to measure these perceptions using survey interviews. Because the study is concerned with influence and decision-making within given subsystems of the community, the positional approach has been used to identify decision-makers. Forty-two local elites in the four policy areas were interviewed, as well as local legislative and executive elites and other local government officials who were fiscally or administratively associated with the operation of the organizations being examined. The interviews were carried out during spring 1969.

The interview schedules consisted of two parts. In the first part each respondent was asked to name the officials (local, state, and federal) who influenced him, whom he influenced, or with whom he shared reciprocal influence relationships. In the second part the respondent was queried as to his perception of the relative influence of local, state, and federal government officials in five areas of organizational activity: funding the organization, establishing standards for professional personnel within the organization, defining the scope of the organization, evaluating the organization in terms of success in meeting its goals, and regulating the organization through legal and administrative channels. This chapter will present the results of the first part of the interview schedule. The second part will be analyzed in later chapters.

The 42 respondents comprise the universe of administrators in the areas of education, law enforcement, social services, and water pollution control, as well as legislative and executive leaders of Onondaga County. These substantive areas were chosen as the four most significant activities with which a local government concerns itself. They comprise the bulk of the budgets and manpower of the relevant governments. Each respondent was asked to give the names of those government officials on the local, state, and federal level of government with whom he considered himself to be in an influence relationship and to evaluate the nature of the relationship. He was asked if he believed that he shared power equally with the official named or, if not, who was dominant in the influence relationship. The relationships were coded as symmetrical (power shared equally by both parties), asymmetrical in favor of respondent (the greatest share of power exercised by the respondent), or asymmetrical in favor of the named official (whom the respondent alleged to hold more power than himself).

To present a comprehensive outline of the perceived influence patterns resulting from analysis of these data and to enable one to make generalizations about influence relations between local, state, and federal actors, a model was used based on the mathematics of digraph theory (theory of directed graphs) as formulated by Steven J. Brams.[1] The assumptions necessary for the use of the Brams' model are as follows:

1. a determination can be made as to which actors have influence over what other actors in a given subsystem;
2. within each pairwise influence relationship, a comparison can be made which will indicate whether the influence is symmetrical or asymmetrical;
3. if the relation is asymmetrical, a determination can be made of the direction of the flow of influence.[2]

Basing the information on the testimony of the actors interviewed, it has been indicated which actors have influence over what others in the system and also whether this influence is symmetrical or asymmetrical. According to Brams, these systems of actors and their influence relations can be considered partly ordered structures because they have elements of both order and disorder. By application of his model, which has been operationalized in a computer program,[3] the elements of order have been clarified and power relations between the actors schematized. When the basic concepts of digraph theory (points and directed lines) are given concrete referents, digraphs can serve as mathematical models of empirical structures; properties of digraphs can be used to draw out structural properties of the empirical world. To quote Brams on the utility of his model,

[after having] defined a political system as something set-theoretic in nature consisting of a set of actors and certain kinds of relations between pairs of actors . . . by relating the actors and their relations to the points and directed lines of a digraph, . . . [one] is able to utilize the findings of digraph theory to highlight some structural properties of the systems under consideration.[4]

Use of this model also allows one to measure the degree of centralization of decision-making and assess the concentration of power in the community examined. This information will enable the drawing of conclusions about the beliefs of local officials regarding their influence relations with state and federal officials. In the case of asymmetrical influence between local, state, and federal actors, it is possible to indicate the one-way direction of flow of influence.

Herbert H. Simon's formulation of asymmetric power relations, and Brams' model, fit this book's conceptualization of power in a community because they enable one to view a community as a network of generally asymmetrical relationships.[5] Simon points up the fact that to speak of the influence of a particular actor upon a community requires specifying whether one means the influence of the actor considered independently, with all the reverse feedback relations ignored, or whether one means the net influence of the actor, taking into account all the reciprocal influences of other actors upon him. Designation of influence relations among actors as symmetrical or asymmetrical enables one to isolate certain feedback relations in the system as a whole. It is assumed that the pattern of feedback relations will tell something about the influence process in the system being examined and thus about the influence relations of local government officials.

## MEASURING THE CONCENTRATION
## OF INFLUENCE

The system analyzed consists of 138 actors, 23 of whom are top-level decision-makers in five functional units of local government in the community: the Onondaga County Department of Social Services, the Onondaga County Department of Public Works, the Onondaga County Sheriff's Department, the Syracuse Police Department, and the Syracuse City School District. Sixteen of the actors are local government officials in the executive and legislative departments of the city of Syracuse and of Onondaga County.* The remaining 96 actors are local, state, and federal government officials whom our respondents stated were in influence relationships with them.**

In applying Brams' model, the first step is measuring the concentration of influence by grouping into mutual influence sets those actors who can influence (directly or indirectly) and be influenced (directly or indirectly) by every other actor within their set. Indirect influence occurs when one actor influences another who in turn influences a third actor. In this case the first indirectly influences the third via his relationship with the second. Indirect influence can be schematized as follows:

---

*The term "general government local official" is being used to describe those local legislative and executive officials who are administratively or fiscally associated with operation of the organization being examined. The term "other local government official" refers to locals in functional areas analogous to but not one of the four being examined.

**Certain respondents said that they were not in influence relationships with anyone. If no other respondents said that they were in influence relationships with these actors, the program categorized them as disconnected. No more mention is made of them. They are NOH, OOC, RAF, SHA, and STR. (See Table 3 for full names of coded actors.)

$$A \rightarrow B \rightarrow C$$

When A influences B and B influences C, A indirectly influences C. If C in turn influences A, then A, B, and C comprise a mutual influence set. Each member of a mutual influence set has either a direct or an indirect reciprocal influence relationship with every other member of the set. These mutual influence sets are defined at a collective level by the above property that all of the sets possess and at an individual level by a list of the members of each set.[6] The sets are disjoint, which means that no actor can be a member of more than one mutual influence set. If there were a common member of more than one mutual influence set, this member would connect together all members of the two sets into a single mutual influence set. In this book's system of influence relationships there are 63 mutual influence sets, one of which contains 69 actors (which shall be refered to as set 69), another contains only 2 actors, and the remaining sets only one actor each. (If an actor does not have any reciprocal influence relationships with other actors, he comprises a set all by himself.)

The mutual influence set can be viewed as a component of the operationalization of the concept of community. Up to this point directly considering the nature of influence relationships between local decision-makers themselves and the implications of this relationship for a concept of community has been avoided. In theoretical terms a community shall be defined as that combination of units and relations (units and relations = system) that perform the major governmental functions having locality relevance.

Influence relations within the community shall be operationalized in terms of a digraph of influence relationships among the members of that community. Examination of the composition of mutual influence sets in the digraph indicates who shares power with whom reciprocally— what sets of actors in a system can influence and be influenced (directly or indirectly) by every other actor in the set. A focal point of the analysis will be the multimember set that contains half of the actors in the system. (See Table 2 for a list of the actors comprising set 69. See Table 3 for the actors and their codes.) Table 1 compares the proportion of local, state, and federal actors in the influence system that are in the set with those that are not.

An inspection of Table 1 shows that the members of set 69—who might be considered the core members of the influence community because of the reciprocal influence relationships that tie them together— are weighted somewhat in favor of local officials relative to their number not in set 69. (The chi-square test indicates that the association between membership in set 69 and level of government of the actor is significant at the 0.05 level, indicating that the distribution of local, state, and federal actors in set 69 and not in set 69 is not

TABLE 1*

Composition of Membership in Set 69,
by Level of Government
(figures in parentheses are percentages
of local, state, and federal actors in system)

| Level | In Set 69 | Not in Set 69 | Total |
|-------|-----------|---------------|-------|
| Local | 39 (67) | 19 (33) | 58 (100) |
| State | 19 (40) | 28 (60) | 47 (100) |
| Federal | 11 (42) | 15 (58) | 26 (100) |
| Total | 69 | 62 | |

*$X^2$ = 8.89 with 2 degrees of freedom p < 0.05; $\lambda$ = 0.21

predictable from the marginal totals. There is a higher proportion
of locals in set 69 relative to their number in the system than of state
and federal actors. This is borne out by the low lambda coefficient.)
Although there are several state and federal officials in this influence
core of the policy-making community, the system does not appear to
be dominated by them. Local officials more than hold their own.

If the mutual influence set is seen as an operational definition
of the core members of an influence community, the findings support
those who have defined community to include vertical relationships
(i.e., between locals and individuals outside of the community) and
the individuals with whom locals have these relationships. The locals
see themselves as exercising at least as much power as their state
and federal counterparts.

Inasmuch as all of the respondents are local government officials,
it could be argued that they will certainly perceive themselves as having
power. The perceptions of locals are being investigated; still, one
wishes to avoid the suggestion of consistent bias present in the data
wherein locals attribute to themselves all of the influence or vice
versa. As will be apparent from the following, locals' attribution of
influence varies with the issue area in question. For example, educators see themselves as far more significant in the making of locality-
relevant decisions than do local law enforcement and water pollution
control officials. One could predict that state and federal officials'
perceptions of the influence they wield would vary by issue area as
well.

Having seen, then, that locals exercise some influence over state
and federal officials, one must examine the questions of the extent of
their influence and in which issue areas. The mathematical model

used here provides a way of assigning metric scores to power relations. Brans calls this an index of power concentration. After grouping the actors studied into their respective mutual influence sets, the remaining influence relations between mutual influence sets are all symmetrical. Since an influence set may be composed of any number of actors, ranging from just one member to the entire set of actors under study, one can speak of the relative concentration of power between sets in terms of the ratio of influencers to influencees. Power is defined as concentrated in the instance when a mutual influence set directly influences one or more other such sets, which together contain a greater number of constituent decision-makers than the influencing set. A set that does exercise such influence is termed a minority control set.[7]

It should be clear that the extent of power concentration, as it is here defined, may show wide variation. While a small number of members may exercise influence over many times their number on the one hand, one may on the other hand also observe power concentration when a mutual influence set of one member controls as few as two other members. Obviously, some method for measuring these differences is desirable. Brams deals with this problem by first arranging the various mutual influence sets in an hierarchical order. The rules for this arrangement are somewhat complex but can be generally indicated as follows. In the top rank of the hierarchy are placed all those mutual influence sets that exercise influence over others and are not themselves subjects of influence. Sets are placed in lower ranks according to the ranks of those sets that exercise influence over them. For example, if one set is influenced by another set in the top rank of the hierarchy, it is placed in level two. If a set is influenced by two different sets, one at the first level and one at the second level, the influenced set is assigned to level 3 of the hierarchy. Those sets in the bottom rank of the hierarchy are those that only receive influence from others. The number of levels of the hierarchy is determined by the pattern of influence among the mutual influence sets. This hierarchical ordering of the 63 mutual influence sets in the study yields five levels, as seen in Figure 2.

Because the system used here contains minority control sets (if it did not, influence could not be considered to be concentrated in Brams' terms ), it is possible to compute Brams' initial index of power concentration (pc) as follows:[8]

$$pc = 1 - \frac{N_{mc}}{N_t} \quad 0 \leq pc \leq 1$$

where

$N_{mc}$ = the number of decision-makers in all minority control sets and

TABLE 2

69 Member Mutual Influence Set

---

## LOCAL

Education
    President, Board of Education
    Member, Board of Education, Syracuse
    Superintendent of Schools, Syracuse School District
    Assistant Superintendent and Executive Assistant to Superintendent, Syracuse School
      District
    Assistant Superintendent for Pupil Personnel, Syracuse School District
    Staff Director of Special Projects, Syracuse School District
Social Services
    Commissioner, Onondaga County Department of Social Services
    Director of Accounting, Onondaga County Department of Social Services
    Director of Personnel and Staff Development, Onondaga County Department of Social
      Services
    Director of Social Services, Onondaga County Department of Social Services
    Director of Child Welfare, Onondaga County Department of Social Services
Law Enforcement
    Chief of Police, Syracuse Police Department
    Captain in charge of Personnel, Syracuse Police Department
    Deputy Chief, Patrol Division, Syracuse Police Department
    First Deputy Chief in Charge of Operations, Syracuse Police Department
    Sheriff of Onondaga County
    Chief Criminal Deputy, Onondaga County Sheriff's Department
Water Pollution Control
    Commissioner of Public Works, City of Syracuse
    Commissioner of Public Works, Onondaga County
    Deputy Commissioner, Division of Engineering, Onondaga County Department of Public
      Works
    Deputy Commissioner, Division of Drainage and Sanitation, Onondaga County Depart-
      ment of Public Works
General Government
    Mayor, City of Syracuse
    President Pro-Tempore and Majority Leader of Common Council, City of Syracuse
    Chairman, Public Safety Committee, Common Council, City of Syracuse
    County Executive, Onondaga County
    Comptroller, Onondaga County
    Chairman, Education and Libraries Committee, Onondaga County Legislature
Other
    Commissioner of Urban Improvement, Department of Urban Improvement, City of
      Syracuse
    Commissioner, Parks Department, City of Syracuse
    Commissioner of Transportation, City of Syracuse
    City Engineer, Department of Engineering, City of Syracuse
    Corporation Counsel, Department of Law, City of Syracuse
    President, Citizen's Housing Council, City of Syracuse
    Executive Director, Human Rights Commission of Syracause and Onondaga County
    District Attorney of Onondaga County
    Commissioner, Onondaga County Department of Personnel
    Commissioner, Onondaga County Department of Mental Hygiene
    Commissioner, Onondaga County Health Department
    Consultant, Maternal and Child Health Bureau, Onondaga County Department of
      Health

---

# STATE

Education
Director, Division of Teacher Education and Certification, New York State Department of Education
Assistant Director, Center on Innovation in Education, New York State Department of Education
Counsel, Office of Counsel, New York State Department of Education
Social Services
Director, Syracuse Area Office, New York State Department of Social Services
Senior Social Services Representative for Child Welfare, Syracuse Area Office, New York State Department of Social Services
Law Enforcement
Director, Division for Local Police and Executive Director, Municipal Police Training Council, Office of Local Government, State of New York
Area Director, New York State Division of Parole
Zone Supervisor of Zone 2, Troop D, New York State Police
Water Pollution Control
Chief, Sewage Facility Section, Bureau of Engineering Design, New York State Department of Health
Director, Bureau of Construction Grants, New York State Department of Health
General Government
Governor, State of New York
Senator, New York State Legislature
Senator, New York State Legislature
Assemblyman, New York State Legislature
Assemblyman, New York State Legislature
Other
Commissioner, New York State Department of Motor Vehicles
Director, Human Rights Division of the State of New York
Director, Municipal Service Division of New York State Civil Service Commission
Chief Alcoholic Beverage Control Investigator, New York State Liquor Authority

# FEDERAL

Education
Commissioner of Education, HEW
Program Management Officer, Area I, New York, Bureau of Elementary and Secondary Education, Office of Education, HEW
Director of Phase C Operations, Educational Professions Development Act Office, HEW
Law Enforcement
Administrator, Law Enforcement Assistance Administration, Department of Justice
Resident Agent for Syracuse, FBI
Federal Jail Inspector, U.S. Bureau of Prisons, Department of Justice
Race and Education Specialist, United States Commission on Civil Rights, Department of Justice
Other
Senator from New York State
Senator from New York State
Congressman from New York State
Traffic Engineering Consultant, Computer Control Traffic, Urban Mass Transportation Administration

## TABLE 3

### Actors and Their Codes

| Code | Actor |
|------|-------|
| ACN | Senior Research Analyst, New York State Department of Audit and Control |
| ARD | Commissioner of Purchase, City of Syracuse |
| BAK | Director of Accounting, Onondaga County Department of Social Services |
| BER | Assistant Superintendent for Pupil Personnel, Syracuse School District |
| BLT | Assemblyman, New York State Legislature |
| CCN | Director, Office of Crime Control Planning, New York State Crime Control |
| CLE | Assistant Superintendent for Instruction, Syracuse School District |
| COO | Chairman, Social Services Committee of County Legislature |
| CWS | Deputy Commissioner, Division of Children's Services, New York State Department of Social Services |
| DBA | Regent, Board of Regents, New York State Department of Education |
| DEF | Commander, Fort Hamilton, United States Army |
| DES | Commissioner, New York State Department of Social Services |
| DEU | Staff Director, Administrative Services, Syracuse School District |
| DPR | Director, Bureau of Data Processing, Department of Finance, City of Syracuse |
| HAN | Chairman, Public Works and Property Committee, Common Council, City of Syracuse |
| HEE | Director of Phase C Operations, Educational Professions Development Act Office, Department of Health, Education and Welfare |
| HEN | Assistant Deputy Commissioner, Division of Drainage and Sanitation, Onondaga County Department of Public Works |
| HEW | Grants Officer, Office of Education, Department of Health, Education and Welfare |
| HOA | Deputy Commissioner of Social Services, Onondaga County Department of Social Services |
| HON | Chairman, Onondaga County Legislature |

| Code | Actor |
|------|-------|
| HSD | Director, Office of Planning and Program Review, Department of Transportation |
| HUJ | Senator from New York State |
| HUM | Assistant Secretary, Model Cities and Governmental Relations, HUD |
| HUP | Director, Division of Program Development and Evaluation, Model Cities and Governmental Relations, HUD |
| HUT | Traffic Engineering Consultant, Computer Control Traffic, Urban Mass Transportation Administration |
| HUU | Assistant Regional Administrator for Model Cities, Model Cities and Governmental Relations, HUD |
| IND | Program Director, Lake Ontario Study of Great Lakes Region, Water Pollution Control Administration, Department of the Interior |
| JAG | Attorney General of the United States Government |
| KAN | Chairman, Public Works Committee, County Legislature |
| LEV | President Pro-Tempore and Majority Leader of Common Council, City of Syracuse |
| MCM | Director of Public Assistance, Onondaga County Department of Social Services |
| MHG | Director, Division of Alcoholism, New York State Department of Mental Hygiene |
| NAP | Deputy Commissioner, Division of Welfare Administration, New York State Department of Social Services |
| NOH | Deputy County Executive of Onondaga County |
| NRD | Director, Department of Representatives, New York State Department of Social Services |
| NRO | Associate Social Services Management Specialist, Syracuse Area Office, New York State Department of Social Services |
| NSS | State Director of Staff Development and Training, New York State Department of Social Services |
| NYA | Commissioner, New York State Department of Audit and Control |
| NYC | Commissioner, New York State Department of Education |
| NYE | Associate Commissioner, Elementary, Secondary, and Adult Education, New York State Department of Education |

| Code | Actor |
|------|-------|
| NYF | Associate Commissioner, Educational Finance and Management Service, New York State Department of Education |
| NYI | Administrator, Educational Practices Act, Inter-Cultural Relations, New York State Department of Education |
| NYU | Director of Urban Education Programs, New York State Department of Education |
| OLG | Director, Office of Local Government |
| OOC | Vice-President of Board of Education, Syracuse |
| PEL | Captain in Charge of Staff Planning, Syracuse Police Department |
| PER | Chairman, New York State Public Employment Relations Board |
| PLA | Director, New York State Office of Planning Coordination |
| POT | Director, Budget Department, City of Syracuse |
| RAF | Chairman, Parks and Recreation Committee, Common Council, City of Syracuse |
| SCS | Director, New York State Department of Correction |
| SES | Employment Services Manager, Human Resources Development Unit, Syracuse District Office, New York Division of Employment |
| SFI | Chairman, Senate Finance Committee, New York State Legislature |
| SHA | Member, Board of Education, Syracuse |
| SIS | Director of Personnel, Department of Personnel, City of Syracuse |
| STR | Chairman, Public Safety Committee of County Legislature |
| TCM | Commissioner of Transportation, Department of Transportation, City of Syracuse |
| TRB | Commissioner of Finance, City of Syracuse |
| TRD | Special Agent, Secret Service, Treasury Department |
| YAH | Chief, Sewage Facility Section, Bureau of Engineering Design, New York State Department of Health |
| YCS | Comptroller, New York State |
| YSH | Director, Bureau of Water and Waste Utilities Management, New York State Department of Health |

$N_t$ = the total number of decision-makers in the political system

The pc is 0.79 between all levels of the hierarchy, indicating a relatively high level of concentration. To give meaning to this value, it is well to explain that, when the number of members of minority control sets is small relative to the total number of members in the political system, control is concentrated in the hands of relatively few of them and the pc is large. (Pc = 1 only when $N_{mc}$ = 0, in which case the many control the few and power is not concentrated.) When the number of members of minority control sets is large relative to the total number of decision-makers, control is concentrated in the hands of a relatively large number of decision-makers, and the pc is small. In this study's system the maximum possible value of pc is 0.99; its minimum possible value is 0.

To discern the position of local decision-makers in what was found to be a relatively concentrated influence network, the composition of minority control sets was analyzed in Table 4. These statistical relationships indicate that the association between level of actor and membership in minority control sets is significant at the 0.05 level. The lambda coefficient indicates that there is no uniform difference between local, state, and federal actors when level of government is compared to membership in minority control sets. The slightly disproportionate number of state officials in minority control sets is not large enough to be statistically significant. In other words, while the few do, on the whole influence the many, the influential few are not significantly discriminated by the level of government at which they exercise their influence.

TABLE 4*

Local, State, and Federal Participants
in Minority Control Sets
(figures in parentheses are percentages of local,
state, and federal actors in system)

| Government Level | In Minority Control Sets | Not in Minority Control Sets | Total |
|---|---|---|---|
| Local | 7 (12) | 51 (88) | 58 (100) |
| State | 15 (32) | 32 (68) | 47 (100) |
| Federal | 4 (15) | 22 (85) | 26 (100) |
| Total | 26 | 105 | 131 |

*$X^2$ = 6.834 with 2 degrees of freedom $p < 0.05$; $\lambda = 0$.

FIGURE 2

Hierarchical Structure of Influence Relations Among All Actors

| | Level of Government | | |
|---|---|---|---|
| Hierarchical Level | Local | State | Federal |
| 1 | Three sets of one actor each:<br>POT<br>HON<br>BER | | |
| 2 | Six sets—one of two actors and the rest of one actor each:<br>BAK-NRO*<br>HAN<br>TRB<br>ARD<br>TCM<br>KAN | Seventeen sets of one actor each:<br>NYA SCS<br>NYC CCN<br>NYF HUJ<br>SES YSH<br>DES YCS<br>CWS PER<br>NAP YAH<br>NRD ACN<br>NSS | |

3    Set 69, containing 23 members and representing the local, state, and federal levels of government. In addition:

| | Local | State | Federal |
|---|---|---|---|
| | Three sets of one actor each:<br>DPR<br>COO<br>DEU | One set consisting of one actor:<br>BLT | |
| 4 | Six sets of one actor each:<br>HOA<br>LEV<br>PEL<br>HEN<br>SIS<br>MCM | Eight sets of one actor each:<br>DBA<br>NYE<br>NYI<br>NYU<br>OLG<br>MHG<br>PLA<br>SFI | Ten sets of one actor each:<br>HEE HUT<br>JAG TRB<br>DEF HUM<br>HUP HUU<br>HSD HEW |
| 5 | one set consisting of one actor:<br>CLE | | one set consisting of one actor:<br>IND |

*BAK is a local official; NRO is a state official

More information about influence concentration between the three levels of government can be gained by examining the concentration of power within the system as one goes from the top of the influence hierarchy to the bottom. The indexes of power concentration between levels have been computed using a refined version of the pc index, as suggested by Brams, which is applicable to all pairs of levels.

$$pc(m,n) = 1 \frac{N_{mc(m)}}{N_{t(m,n)} - N_{u(m,n)}} \quad \text{if } N_{mc(m)} > 0$$

$$pc(m,n) = 0 \qquad\qquad\qquad \text{if } N_{mc(m)} = 0$$

where $0 \leq pc(m,n) < 1$ and

$N_{c(m)}$ = the number of decision-makers in minority control sets at level m,

$N_{t(m,n)}$ = the total number of decision-makers in the political system at levels m through n,

$N_{u(m,n)}$ = the number of decision-makers (not in minority control sets at level m) at levels m through n uninfluenced by any minority control sets at level m.[9]

As Table 5 indicates, power is concentrated (i.e., pc $\geq$ 0.5) only between levels 1 and 2 and levels 2 and 3. Levels 3 and 4 and 4 and 5 have a pc of 0 because there are no minority control sets at levels 3 and 4. The top three levels, those between which power is concentrated, contain a majority of actors in the system (105 out of 131).

Table 6 shows the totals, and percentages of the total numbers, of local, state, and federal government influentials found at levels 1 and 2, level 3, and levels 4 and 5. Levels have been combined because levels 1 and 2 and levels 4 and 5 contain so few actors.

TABLE 5

Indexes of Power Concentration Between All
Adjacent Levels in the System

| Level | pc(m,n) |
|-------|---------|
| 1,2 | 0.5 |
| 2,3 | 0.71 |
| 3,4 | 0.00 |
| 4,5 | 0.00 |

TABLE 6*

Local, State, and Federal Actors,
by Hierarchical Level
(figures in parentheses are percentages
of local, state, and federal actors in system)

| Hierarchical | Level of Government | | | |
|---|---|---|---|---|
| Level | Local | State | Federal | Total |
| 1 and 2 | 8 (13) | 19 (42) | 4 (15) | 31 |
| 3 | 45 (75) | 18 (40) | 11 (42) | 74 |
| 4 and 5 | 7 (12) | 8 (18) | 11 (42) | 26 |
| Total | 60 (100) | 45 (100) | 26 (100) | |

*$X^2$ = 23.79 with 4 degrees of freedom p < 0.01; $\lambda$ = 0.02.

The chi-square test indicates that the association between level assignment and level of actor is significant at the 0.01 level. The lambda
coefficient indicates that there is not a uniform difference between
local, state, and federal actors when level of government is compared
to hierarchical level assignment. Compared to their distribution in
the system, state actors are overrepresented at the top levels and
local actors predominate at the middle level. The bottom levels
contain a large share of only the federal officials. The structural
pattern emerging from this analysis of the perceptions of local officials
is that the vast majority of local and federal decision-makers (87 percent of the local officials and 84 percent of the federal officials) are
at levels 3, 4, or 5 and thus the object of minority control from higher
levels, whereas less than half of the state decision-makers are at
levels 3, 4, and 5. Local and federal actors are the objects of minority
control in more cases than are state officials.

The preliminary findings about the total system under study can
be summarized as follows. From the testimony of locals interviewed,
the vertical dimension of community power is very important. They
see themselves in a rich mixture of one-way and mutual influence
relationships with officials at state and federal levels. It was found
that a greater percentage of state officials than of local or federal
officials are the members of minority control sets. Local and federal
decision-makers are more frequently found in sets directly influenced
by minority control sets than are state officials. (To recapitulate, a
minority control set by definition is a mutual influence set that directly
influences one or more other mutual influence sets containing a total
of more constituent decision-makers.) No indication that this pattern

indicates a clear-cut domination of local levels of activity was found,
however. Locals are found in significant numbers is the most salient
feature of the influence system, the large mutual influence set containing over half of the actors in the system. Likewise, they are prominently represented in the numerous minority control sets, though not
so prominently as state officials, which give the system its overall
high degree of power concentration. Furthermore, local officials are
by no means "buried" at the bottom of the influence hierarchy. These
are conclusions based on an analysis cutting across the four functional
categories of government activity studied. The investigation of the
influence relationships within each of these four categories will now
be presented.

## INFLUENCE RELATIONS IN FOUR FUNCTIONS
## OF LOCAL GOVERNMENT

Within the education subsystem there are six hierarchical levels,
but they contain no mutual influence sets that consist of more than one
actor. Analyzing the composition of minority control sets, one finds
no significant association ($p > 0.05$) between level of government of
actor and membership in a minority control set. This suggests that
educators see themselves as sharing influence with state and federal
officials and not as subservient to them. If anything they share power
with state and federal officials even more than the "norm" for the
total system.

Despite the lack of influence predominance of any one level of
government in education, it is interesting to examine individually the
actors at the top levels in the hierarchical structure (not shown here).
At level 1 are found two local educators and a fiscal officer of the
New York State Department of Education. They are the superintendent
of the Syracuse School District, the assistant superintendent second
in position to the superintendent, and the director of the Audit and
Control Division of the New York State Department of Education
(NYSDE). Furthermore, only the superintendent of schools exercises
minority control. He is the number one man with respect to his organization both horizontally (in terms of general government locals) and
vertically (in terms of state and federal decision-makers relevant to
education).

At level 2 are two local officials, three state officials, and one
federal official. They are the assistant superintendent in charge of
pupil personnel, an official of the City Health Department, the NYSDE's
director of the office of counsel, an official of its Urban Aid to Education office, and the U.S. Department of Health, Education, and Welfare
(HEW) commissioner of education. The general government locals

included are the chairman of the Board of Education at level 3 and the commissioner of finance of the city of Syracuse at level 4. (The corresponding budgetary official of the NYSDE is at level 1.) If the hierarchy is examined with regard to the individuals comprising it, certain locals stand out. This is a useful finding but does not override the conclusion that local, state, and federal actors share quite equally influence in education at the local level.

The social welfare subsystem (a function of county as opposed to city government) offers a sharp contrast to the education subsystem. Two general government officials, the county executive and the county budget director, are at level 1 of the social services hierarchy, while the corresponding officials for education are at levels 3 and 4 of the education hierarchy. The commissioner of social services is at a lower hierarchical level than the county executive. The superintendent of schools, however, is at level 1 and the chairman of the Board of Education at level 3. The mayor of the city of Syracuse does not appear in the education or the social welfare subsystems. Neither he nor the educators and social welfare workers believe that he is in any kind of an influence relationship with them. The social welfare subsystem is similar to the education subsystem in regard to fiscal matters. The budgetary official of the New York State Department of Social Services is at level 2 and the corresponding State Education Department official at level 1.

Analysis of the hierarchical level assignments of actors in social welfare shows that there is no significant association between level assignment and level of government. The composition of minority control sets indicates that while power is more concentrated in the social welfare subsystem than in either the entire system or the education subsystem, local officials attain minority control status with about the same frequency as do state and federal officials.

The perceptions of local law enforcement decision-makers indicate that they are unlike education and social welfare officials in that they see themselves as secondary to relevant decision-makers at the state and federal levels of government. Hierarchical assignment of actors in the law enforcement subsystem yields six levels. All four of the actors at levels 1 and 2 represent the state and federal governments. Each of these actors constitutes a mutual influence set that is also a minority control set. These data taken with a high pc (0.84) for the subsystem indicate that power is concentrated in the hands of state and federal decision-makers. One does not find local government officials until level 4, where the only mutual influence set in the subsystem containing more than one actor was found. Locals included in this set are the county sheriff, the Syracuse police chief, two other high-ranking officers of the Syracuse Police Department, the chairman of the Public Safety Committee of the County Legislature, the county comptroller, the county budget director, and the commissioner of finance of the city of Syracuse. As suggested above, a mutual influence set consisting of many actors may be considered the core influence system among the members of a community.

An analysis of the composition of this 15-member mutual influence set, located at level 4 in the hierarchy, shows that half of the locals in the law-enforcement subsystem are members of the set but only 17 percent of the state and federal officials included in the subsystem are members of the set. The minority control sets at higher levels, on the other hand, are composed of five state and federal officials and only two local government officials. This is consistent with the previous conclusion that power is relatively concentrated in the hands of state and federal decision-makers in law enforcement.

In conformity with common-sense notions of state and federal influence on the activities of local governments, water pollution abatement in Onondaga County is, of the four governmental functions examined, most affected by outside decision-makers. Those locals operating the water pollution abatement program are influenced almost exclusively by decision-makers at higher levels of government. The pattern of influence relations is such that local individuals neither receive influence from their fellow local officials nor do they influence state and federal officials. Of the seven actors at the top level of the hierarchy, six are New York State Department of Health officials. The only local sharing this level is the Onondaga County commissioner of public works. In a three-level hierarchy all but two of the five locals included are at the third and bottom level. The only elected local official to appear in the hierarchy is the county executive. He appears at level 3, influencing no one but influenced by the deputy commissioner of the Onondaga County Public Works Department.

## CONCLUSION

Figure 3 summarizes the findings. For the entire system the hypothesis most strongly supported by the data is that of the symmetry of influence relations between locals and state and federal officials. This conclusion is based on all issue areas taken together. As evident in Figure 3, there are major differences among issue areas. In education and social welfare locals see themselves as having an equal share with their state and federal counterparts in the making of decisions relevant to their area. Locals in water pollution control and in law enforcement believe that they are secondary to those at higher levels. These differences by functional area are the most significant findings.

Having made a determination of the direction of influence relationships between and among local, state, and federal officials, the

FIGURE 3

Summary of Influence Relations

| | Entire System | Education | Social Service | Law Enforcement | Water Pollution Abatement |
|---|---|---|---|---|---|
| Multimember influence sets ("community") | 1 of 69 members comprising half of the actors in the system<br><br>60 percent of the locals in the system are included, 40 percent of the state actors in system, and 42 percent of the federal actors | none | none | 1 of 15 members comprising one-third of the actors in the subsystem | none |
| Summary of hierarchical ordering by level of government | a. locals predominate at middle level<br><br>b. state officials overrepresented at top levels<br><br>c. lowest levels contain large share of federal officials only | no significant differences in hierarchical level assignment based on level of actor | no significant differences in hierarchical level assignment based on level of actor | a. locals concentrated at middle level<br><br>b. state and federal officials overrepresented at top levels | a. majority of locals at bottom level<br><br>b. state and federal at top level |
| Indexes of power concentration | 0.79 | 0.76 | 0.81 | 0.84 | 0.47 |
| Analysis of composition of minority control sets | slightly greater number of state officials than of local and federal officials are in minority control sets | local officials share minority control status equally with state and federal officials | local officials share minority control status equally with state and federal officials | significantly greater number of state and federal officials than of local officials are in minority control sets | with one exception all minority control actors are state and federal officials |

authors believe that the findings require some modification of theories of community power. This study began with the recognition that students of community power have not systematically investigated the extent to which power is exercised at the local level, though speculation abounds that encroaching state and federal governments, combined with the financial dependency of local governments, have rendered locals powerless. It was thought that the survey data would indicate power-lessness on the part of local officials. In the course of interviewing it became increasingly clear that locals in Onondaga County differ in their assessments of their influence according to the area of government with which they are involved. Educators and social service officials acknowledge being dominated by some state and federal officials but at the same time see themselves as dominant in their relations with other extracommunity officials.

In searching for an explanation of this perceived equality of influence between educators and social service workers and state and federal officials, it is useful to look again at the two areas of govern-ment individually. Local educators believe that they exercise more influence in the making of top-level policy decisions than do general government locals or state and federal officials. For example, the superintendent of schools in Syracuse expressed his conviction that he carried a great share of the responsibility for guiding the process of adjusting to new demands and attempting solutions to old problems in urban education. This, taken with similar expressions of the belief in personal responsibility for what happens in the Syracuse school system, makes the findings understandable.

Social service locals expressed less conviction than educators as to their latitude in decision-making. At the same time, they ex-pressed a desire to have all power over the public welfare function taken away from the county government—along with all fiscal respon-sibility. Despite the social service locals' allegiance to the traditional bureaucratic virtues of deference to those above them in a formal hierarchy, they claimed to have leverage with the New York State Department of Social Services.

For the police the usual insistence that the community is not the locus of power is true in the minds of law enforcers themselves. Those officials involved in water pollution control also see their role in decision-making as secondary to that of state and federal officials. The reasons for this are different for each of these two functions. In the case of law enforcement the state and federal judiciary is said by locals to have seriously curtailed their role in decision-making by imposing restraints on operating procedures. The state and federal executive departments and legislatures offer assistance in technical matters but have not challenged the autonomy of locals to any signifi-cant extent. Locals see their relationship with state and federal law enforcers as a cooperative enterprise that is marked by very little conflict.

The Law Enforcement Assistance Administration of the Department of Justice was created to assist localities and does just that. The Federal Bureau of Investigation (FBI), including its resident agent in Syracuse, has no jurisdiction over locals. Again, it is a cooperative relationship marked by mutual give and take. Several bureaus and divisions of New York State government offer similar kinds of assistance in a similarly noncoercive way. In sum, locals believe that they should have administrative authority for enforcing the law, but the courts have seriously infringed upon their authority.

Water control people differ in that they believe that their function is best administered from the top down. In most cases they are professionals in engineering who interact on a professional basis with those at higher levels of government. They do not resent decision-making from above because the scope of their activity is not generically local. The physical boundaries with which they are concerned (i.e., a watershed, a lake, a river system) do not coincide with a specific local government's jurisdiction. Their function differs from that of law enforcement in terms of funding as well. The locality pays practically all of the cost of maintaining a police or sheriff's department. The state and federal governments pay the greatest share of the costs of water pollution control. The source of funding appears to have a direct relationship to the resentment or lack of resentment locals feel over state and federal involvement in decision-making.

What all this means in terms of the community is that some locals believe that they have a valid share in the making of decisions relevant to their public lives. Others see themselves as reactors to higher-level policy-makers rather than an integral part of the policy-making process. More generally, it is obvious that the vertical dimension ought not be ignored by students of power in the community. The community must be redefined to include its vertical axis if concepts of power and influence are to be realistically tested. As John Walton and others have suggested, the locality itself consists of many sub-systems that are parts of larger systems.[10] Economic units within the locality are an example of this conceptualization. General Electric has plants in Syracuse. They are readily viewed as parts of a larger whole. The same is true of units and subunits of local government. The Onondaga County Department of Social Services, for example, must be viewed as part of a larger system that includes the New York State Department of Social Services as well as applicable federal agencies. Similarly, the executive department of the city of Syracuse can best be understood when its connection to state and federal governments are made clear. HEW and the Department of Housing and Urban Development (HUD) on the federal level, the Office of Local Government,

and the Department of Transportation are only a few of the vertical
parameters of the mayor's interactive network.

The direct relationship between HEW, HUD, the Department of
Justice, and the Department of the Interior and departments of the
governments of the city of Syracuse and of Onondaga County suggest
that the nature of the U.S. federal system, insofar as Syracuse, New
York, is concerned, is indeed no longer a tripartite system with lines
of communication exclusively from federal, to state, to local but rather
a fluid system with professionals at the local level interacting directly
with professionals in corresponding substantive areas on the state and
federal levels. The Syracuse superintendent of schools, for example,
believes himself to be in influence relationships, some symmetrical,
some asymmetrical in his or the other's direction, with a number of
individuals within HEW, including the commissioner. The locals interact with state people more frequently than with federal people and their
interaction with state officials is more likely to be asymmetrical in
the state officials' favor, yet one cannot conclude that the local inter-
acts only with state officials and that the state officials call the shots
in every case. Variance from one functional area to another is great,
as has been seen. Still, the overall conclusion is that locals constitute
an integral part of the federal system of governance.

The facts of variance between functional areas lead to the conclusion that the pluralist models of community power have more relevance
to what was found in Syracuse than do the elitist models. The respondents either believed that they made the decisions relevant to their
areas or that they knew who did make the decisions. A further study
would certainly examine the economic and social, as well as the
political, subsystems of the community.

## AN UNOBTRUSIVE MEASURE
## OF COMMUNITY POWER

This study has focused on an analysis of local government officials' influence relations with each other and with state and federal
officials involved in corresponding policy areas.  The generalizations
advanced so far have relied on the limited basis of testimony of the
individuals involved.  The conclusions here do not represent anything
more than the views, recollections, observations, and perceptions of
government leaders in Onondaga County.  A study of this sort epitomizes
"obtrusiveness" as the term is defined by Eugene Webb et al.[1]  Many
confounding variables are introduced in the assessment of power by
the intrusion of the personality of the respondent generated by the
presence of the interviewer.  Recognizing this limitation, an additional
measure of power has been employed that is independent of the views,
recollections, observations, and perceptions of the actors themselves.
By examining the respondents' appointment calendars their nongovernmental community, local general government, state government, and
federal government contacts have been tallied and analyzed  for a
given period of time.  It is realized that this measure is not comprehensive enough to be the mainstay of an investigation of power.
It is meant only as an unobtrusive check on our primary method of
gaining insight into the problem posed by the study.

It is interesting to note that a discussion of former New York
Police Commissioner Howard Leary's "brilliant political maneuvering"
highlights the fact that, in managing to keep one step ahead of a staff
made up of hard-bitten career policemen, Mr. Leary "confounded their
usual sources of information by insisting upon keeping his own appointment book."  According to this commentator, Mr. Leary took
his appointment book with him when he left his office and thus his top
commanders rarely knew where he was or whom he saw and how
much he knew of their doings.[2]

The appointment entries were categorized as local other (non-government community group or individual), local general government, state government, and federal government. In addition, it was noted whether the meeting took place at the respondent's office, the other's office, or on neutral territory (some place other than the offices of those involved in the meeting). It was assumed that the movement of these government officials would indicate something about the influence relationships between them. Theories of social interaction among members of a group permit one to consider two actors to be in a power relationship when they appear to be responsive to each other's behavior.[3] The behavior was coded as symmetrical or asymmetrical by noting where the meeting between each pair of actors took place. Thus, a preponderance of meetings between local and state people that are held in the offices of the state people suggest that influence is asymmetrical in the direction of state officials. The official that visits another more frequently than he is visited by that other can be assumed to be in an asymmetrical influence relationship. The relationship would be coded as asymmetrical in the other's favor. If the number of visits is equally divided between the respondents' offices, the others' offices, and neutral territory, it can be assumed that power is symmetrical. In the following pages the results of the analyses of the appointment calendar and interview data will be presented and compared.

The appointment calendar data was looked at in two ways. First, it was attempted to discern a relationship between the level of government of the person being met with and the location of the meeting. Profiles of the distribution of visits between the four categories of those visited were then developed. There is not appointment calendar information for all of the respondents. Most of the general government locals interviewed hold their government post in addition to a full-time occupation. Their appointment calendars reflect their daily business as well as government contacts, and it was thought that it would be presumptuous to ask to peruse them. Appointment calendar information for only those general government locals who hold their posts on a full-time basis is used. Furthermore, some functional area respondents either did not keep appointment calendars or refused to allow access to them. Table 7 shows the number of sets of appointment calendar data available and unavailable for each group of respondents. The data are not adequate to make conclusions about law enforcers or general government locals as groups.

This phase of the study was primarily concerned with the interrelations between local, state, and federal actors involved in the same functional areas. In deference to the community power literature the interaction between government officials and nongovernment community groups and individuals was looked at briefly. The respondents

TABLE 7

Number of Sets of Appointment Calendar Data
Available and Unavailable for Each Group of
Respondents

|  | Education | Social Service | Law En- forcement | Water Pol- lution Abatement | General Government Locals |
|---|---|---|---|---|---|
| Available | 7 | 5 | 1 | 2 | 3 |
| Unavailable | 0 | 2 | 6 | 0 | 13 |

were asked whether they believed other government officials or non-government locals to be more influential to their decision-making. Seventy-five percent of the respondents said that other government officials are more significant. The appointment calendar data provide a measure of the influence of local others vis-à-vis the respondents. This relationship shall be pointed out as the appointment calendar data is analyzed.

Table 8 shows the distribution of entries among all individuals. The greatest number of contacts is with local others and general government locals, with 35 and 36 percent, respectively. State and federal contacts accounted for 31 and 8 percent, respectively. Visits with local others are evenly divided between the respondent's office, the other's office, and neutral territory. Visits with general government locals, state officials, and federal officials occur most frequently at their offices, as Table 9 shows. Fifty-six percent of visits with general government locals are at their offices, 85 percent of visits with state officials are at their offices, and 41 percent of visits with federal officials are at their offices. This suggests that influence relations between the respondents and general government locals and state officials are asymmetrical in the direction of the others. Visits with federal officials occur at the other's office only slightly more frequently.

Looking at educators individually, one finds that the greatest number of their contacts are with local others and general government locals. Eighty percent are with state and federal officials. The greatest share of visits with general government locals and state officials is at their offices. The greatest number of federal visits is divided between their offices and neutral territory. Relations between educators and general government locals and state officials are asymmetrical in the direction of the others. Influence relations between educators and federal officials are symmetrical.

TABLE 8*

Distribution of Entries

| Location | Local Others | General Government | State | Federal |
|----------|--------------|--------------------|-------|---------|
| Respondent's office | 48 | 32 | 5 | 9 |
| Other's office | 42 | 86 | 77 | 14 |
| Other | 57 | 35 | 9 | 11 |
| Total | 147 | 153 | 91 | 34 |

*$x^2 = 74$; d.f. = 6; $p < 0.01$; $\lambda = 0.14$.

TABLE 9

Percentages of Visits in Respondent's Office,
Other's Office, and Neutral Territory

| Location | Local Others | General Government | State | Federal |
|----------|--------------|--------------------|-------|---------|
| Respondent's office | 33 | 21 | 5 | 27 |
| Other's Office | 28 | 56 | 85 | 41 |
| Neutral | 39 | 23 | 10 | 32 |
| Total | 100 | 100 | 100 | 100 |

Unlike educators, social service officials have an equal number of visits with local and state officials. The number of federal visits is small. Over half of the visits with local others are on neutral territory. Thirty-five percent are at the other's office, and only 9 percent at the respondent's office. Forty-one percent of visits with general government locals are on neutral territory, 50 percent at the other's office, and again only 9 percent at the respondent's office. The pattern of asymmetry in the direction of the other is more pronounced in the case of state officials. Here, 97 percent of the visits are at the other's office and only 3 percent on neutral territory. None are at the office of the local social service officials. Over half of their visits with local others took place on neutral territory. The conclusion is that influence relations with local others are symmetrical. Eighty percent of visits with general government locals and 100 percent

of visits with state officials took place at the other's office. This
suggests that influence relations are asymmetrical in the direction
of the general government local and the state official. The number
of visits with federal officials is too small to make conclusions.

To aid in making comparisons among the three groups, Table
10 was constructed. There is not a very great disparity in distribution
of visits by function. Perhaps the only distinction of note is in the
percentage of visits devoted to state officials. Social service officials
devote 48 percent and water control 5 percent. Educators devote a
greater percentage of visits to local others and to federal officials than
do either social service or water control officials, but this may reflect
the fact that during the time span of the sample educators were attempting to convince Syracusans of the merits of a radical reorganiza-
tion of all elementary school facilities.

Visits with general government locals and with state officials
most frequently take place at the office of the other. Visits with
federal officials are evenly divided between neutral territory and the
office of the other. The conclusion is that influence relations between
educators, social service officials, water pollution control officials,
and general government locals and state officials are asymmetrical
in favor of the others. Influence relations with federal officials are
symmetrical.

The purpose of the foregoing look at appointment calendar data
was to see to what extent an unobtrusive measure correlates with
perceptions of influence of actors in a political system. The correlation is not very great. In comparing the interview data and the appointment calendar data two ratios for each actor in the political
system were computed. One was the ratio of visits in the respondents'
office over the total number of visits minus those occuring on neutral

TABLE 10

Distribution of Visits, by Function

| Position | Local Others Number | Per-cent | General Government Number | Per-cent | State Number | Per-cent | Federal Number | Per-cent |
|---|---|---|---|---|---|---|---|---|
| Educators | 98 | 50 | 60 | 30 | 25 | 13 | 14 | 7 |
| Social service officials | 23 | 23 | 22 | 22 | 48 | 48 | 7 | 7 |
| Water control officials | 9 | 26 | 15 | 43 | 5 | 14 | 6 | 17 |

territory. The other, taken from the interview data, was the ratio of the number of people the respondent influences (including those with whom he is in a symmetrical influence relationship) over the number of people who influence him. The correlation between these two variables is 0.24. This is consistent with the discrepancy in the findings. The appointment calendar data indicate generally asymmetrical relations between locals and the various groups with which they were compared.

The hypothesis most strongly supported by the interview data was that of the symmetry of influence relations between locals and state and federal officials. This conclusion is based on all issue areas taken together. There are major differences according to issue area. In education and social welfare locals see themselves as having an equal share with their state and federal counterparts in the making of decisions relevant to their area. Locals in water pollution control and in law enforcement believe that they are secondary to those at higher levels. These differences by functional area were the most significant findings based on the interview data.

The respondents think that they share equally in influence but the unobtrusive measure suggests that they do not. Perhaps the most clear-cut consequence of the findings is further support for those who argue that power is not a static attribute of actors but a multidimensional phenomenon that must be evaluated contextually. More specifically, the study supports the following propositions:

1. Government officials tend to perceive themselves as more powerful than objective indicators of power would seem to warrant. While many people may feel themselves powerless and alienated, this does not appear to be true of the government officials that were interviewed. Correctly or incorrectly, they see themselves as relatively influential in their dealings with others. Furthermore, this disparity in the findings might be explained by the fact that on a day-to-day basis respondents are perhaps able to modify extracommunity rules and regulations—that is, to exert influence. But on special critical and/or ritualistic occasions when meetings take place, the higher level officials are given deference by having people go to their office.

2. Power relations are relative not only as between political actors but also from one issue area to another. Both the measure of perceived power and the unobtrusive measure showed that officials in different functional areas had widely differing influence relations with others. There tended to be more similarity in influence position among members of a functional area than between the issue areas.

This suggests, once again, that one must not only ask about power with respect to whom but also power to accomplish what goals. When observers question the power of community groups vis-à-vis

outside forces, they must not ignore the possibility that people within
the community may be powerful on some issues and weak on others.
No single indicator is likely to result in an accurate measure of power.
The conclusion here is that this phase of the study not only suggests
the complexity of power relations but also demonstrates the advantages
of the use of a variety of measures that can systematically uncover
and help analyze the important and many-sided question of power in
American communities.

## THE STUDY OF PUBLIC OPINION

In this part of the study are presented the results of the investigation of the way residents of the metropolitan area order priorities for government action. After taking a stratified random sample of the population of Syracuse, an open selection technique was used to assess each respondent's set of urban priority preferences. As reported in Part III, it was then attempted to discern the extent to which these priorities are felt by local government.

Although the term "public opinion" was not used until the eighteenth century, the phenomenon itself was noted and described by writers in ancient, medieval, and early modern times. Political theorists such as Plato, Aristotle, Machiavelli, and Rousseau noted the importance of what might be called mass opinion. Through the fifteenth, sixteenth, and seventeenth centuries, the invention of the printing press, the Renaissance, and the discovery of new lands helped to enlarge the reading public and expand the arena of public opinion. In the eighteenth and nineteenth centuries the struggle for parliamentary forms of government and the extension of suffrage led to the establishment of institutions and processes appropriate to the view that the public should in some way participate in the decisions of the state. By the end of the first quarter of the nineteenth century the concept of public opinion had entered the mainstream of political theory.

The ethical imperative that a government heed the opinion of its people has its origins in democratic ideology. Early students of the concept felt that it had mystical or divine properties, but they also recognized its importance as an instrument of social control and as the main safeguard against the abuse of power. Toward the end of the nineteenth century public opinion was suggested to be the foundation of all government:

Yet opinion has really been the chief and ultimate power
in nearly all nations at nearly all times. I do not mean
merely the opinion of the class to which the rulers belong
. . . I mean the opinion, unspoken, unconscious, but not
the less real and potent, of the masses of the people.
Governments have always rested, and, special cases
apart, must rest, if not on the affection, then on the rev-
erence or awe, if not on the active approval, then on the
silent acquiescence of the numerical majority. [1]

As public influence over government grew through new processes of
participation, it became increasingly important to recognize what the
public was thinking. No leader could maintain himself long if he
ignored the opinions of his people.

The twentieth century witnessed a tremendous expansion of
interest in public opinion and marked the end of the political writers'
dominance in studying the field. Social scientists generally made a
broad frontal attack on the subject, bringing new interests and new
perspectives to the study. Sociologists extended the understanding
of the process of opinion formation. The press was recognized as a
molder and reflector of popular opinion. Social psychologists examined
the content and motivation of opinion and sought to determine the role
of the personality and the group in opinion formation. Historians and
political scientists studied the political role of public opinion and the
nature of the relation of opinion to policy-making and law. Although
from the start there was little agreement about the virtue and competence of public opinion, such studies did lead to greater understanding
of its nature and role.

The alleged role public opinion and its manipulation played in
events preceding and during World War I aroused a continuing interest
in new dimensions of public opinion and in the relation between opinion
and propaganda. The decade of the 1920s probably marks the beginning
of what may be called the modern study of public opinion. The war
stimulated a number of studies on morale, discipline, and leadership,
and psychologists applied new techniques of educational and intelligence
testing in screening soldiers. These new operations led to the development of new questionnaire techniques and machines for the tabulation
of large quantities of data. They may have been the basis for the
widespread interest in statistical studies of public opinion and in
attempts to measure opinion with quantitative methods. [2]

The 1930s brought continued theoretical interest in public
opinion and the establishment of public opinion courses in higher
education. There was expanded interest in pressure groups, propaganda, mass communication, government information agencies, public
opinion measurement and theory, the psychology of opinion formation,

and many other aspects of public opinion. The mid-1930s brought the advent of modern scientific opinion polling, with sampling techniques to assure reliable representative opinions. In 1937 appeared the first issue of the Public Opinion Quarterly, the first journal devoted exclusively to the expanding field of public opinion. Complementing this publication was the Journalism Quarterly, which reported systematically the growing research in the field of mass communications.

The decade of the 1940s brought a new literature, marking a changed emphasis away from theoretical study toward the practical application of theories. The pollsters stimulated interest in sampling and interviewing techniques, the question of the competence of the public, and the role of opinion in governmental decision-making. Students of public opinion, public relations, and propaganda analysis manned a growing number of governmental information agencies. The media, national and international psychological warfare, advertising, and polling were carefully studied through content analysis.

The last two decades have witnessed extended analysis of several traditional issues. Techniques of polling, surveying, and data analysis have received much attention. The effects of both personal and environmental actors on the formation of public opinion have been the objects of renewed study, with a number of sociological reports penetrating quite deeply the public opinion implications of elites, motivation, and decision-making. The media, especially television, have attracted the concern of many, frequently to the question of media effects, especially on children, and to the problem of the public and social responsibility of the media and the national news services. Interest in the study of public opinion abroad has also become widespread. The attitudes and opinions of the public, as well as of its leaders, have been surveyed, and comparative studies have also been made.

There are many reasons for the increasing interest in public opinion outlined above. The spread of democracy and the extension of the vote are important factors. Historically, political theorists have recognized the link between opinion and government, and modern-day politicians have developed and extended a number of devices not only for sounding out but also for shaping constituent opinion. As the voting public enlarges, it becomes more powerful, and efforts to influence it and win its support become more intense.

Expanding educational opportunity has also contributed to the increasing concern with public opinion. Education tends to raise hopes, to increase demands, and to induce and encourage the expression of opinion that, as a result of education, is becoming more competent. Improvements in transportation and communication systems have also enhanced the importance of public opinion by expanding the size and diversity of publics as well as by facilitating intercourse among those publics. Those who control the media have the power to move opinion; those who do not have less influence. Public opinion itself has become more influential as the media tend to mobilize, unify, and, to some extent, standardize attitudes and beliefs.

The struggle to win public opinion support has also intensified the concern for public opinion. The new industrial state, with its emphasis on mass production and mass consumption and its require- ments of industrial concentration and consumer advertising, epitomizes this struggle in the economic sphere.[3] In the political sphere the struggle for public opinion goes on among nations, groups and blocs, and parties and pressure groups and is accompanied by propaganda, national and international broadcasts, and huge campaign expenditures, all in the name of public support. In the governmental sphere public opinion is increasingly important because the carrying-out of so many public policies necessitates the support and cooperation of large numbers of people. Such support on a broad scale is needed to imple- ment public policies in nondemocratic as well as in democratic countries. Even in the least democratic regime opinion may influence the direction and tempo of policy, raising to unprecedented proportions the responsibility of government to obtain opinion leadership.[4] The problems of authority and freedom, especially in the political sphere, but also in the economic and social realms, present critical issues in the area of public opinion.

The relation between power and public opinion, as basic as it is to early conceptions of public opinion, remain vague and complex. Early simplistic notions that public opinion had mystical or divine properties were encouraged by the flourishing of democratic ideologies during the eighteenth century and saw public opinion as a consensus among a large number of people that somehow exercised force. More recently, students have been able to identify a number of distinguishing characteristics of public opinion, as shall be seen, but its role in the policy-making process is still not clear. Government policies and all important historical events, one writer suggests, are shaped by the opinions of the members of the political community involved. That is the reason for interest in public opinion. The resolution of public issues is influenced in one way or another by the sentiments of the public, although the influence is often circuitous and hard to discern.[5]

If ever there existed a direct link between opinion and policy, it has been in recent decades, during which the relations between govern- ment and public opinion have been radically transformed. The means for informing and influencing the public have undergone extensive changes. The loci of power in society, always transitory and dispersed in the past, have become centralized and concentrated. The growth in scope and complexity of governmental functions has increasingly bewildered and alienated the average man, with public policy questions more and more removed from his range of knowledge and experience.

The question directing this study involves the interrelationship of public opinion, power, and policy-making. After exploring some characteristics of public opinion and examining its measurement, the connection between opinion and power will be discussed in more detail, followed by comments on the results of an opinion survey concerning metropolitan priorities. The policy-making process itself will be considered in the last section of this book, at which time it is hoped that the three concepts—power, public opinion, and policy-making—can be reconciled.

## WHAT IS PUBLIC OPINION?

Much like the discussion of power, the concept of public opinion has suffered from vague yet stylish erudition. There are almost as many definitions of public opinion as there are writers on the subject. Public opinion has been called the "queen of the world," the Voice of God," "a powerful, bold, and unmeasurable party," and "that great compound of folly, weakness, prejudice, wrong feeling, right feeling, obstinacy, and newspaper paragraphs."[6]

Public opinion is considered an influential factor in human affairs, but scholars are obliged to recognize its amorphous and fluid quality. As one author remarks, "Public opinion has come to refer to a sort of secular idol, and is a 'god-term' to which citizens, scientists, and office-holders alike pay allegiance, partly as a condition of sanctity."[7] In spite of differences in definition students of public opinion generally agree at least that it is a collection of individual opinions on an issue of public interest, and they usually note that these opinions can exercise influence over individual behavior, group behavior, and government policy.

The term may be used to refer to any collection of individual opinion. If one could suggest that there was one such group to which the term public opinion always referred, the problem of definition would be much simpler. In fact, early political theorists generally assumed that the term was limited to the political opinion of the community. This assumption is not valid, however, for the number of publics is large and varied, and attempts to find "the public" are generally arbitrary and fruitless. The study of public opinion is, therefore, the study of collections of individual opinions wherever they may be found.

An opinion may be defined as a verbal expression of attitudes. In the human context, an attitude is the posture a person adopts in relation to his environment, a predisposition to respond in a particular manner to particular objects in the environment.[8] One learns the nature of an individual's attitudes when he manifests them in actions

or verbal opinions. But words are by no means the only expressions
of attitudes; consider laughs, frowns, rage, or tears. And not all
verbal statements are necessarily opinions. Some writers speak of
latent or internal public opinion, suggesting that expression is not
essential. This idea complicates the concept of public opinion, however, since unexpressed thoughts or attitudes, though they may have
some influence, are private opinions and must be expressed in some
fashion to become public opinion. Thus, the different forms an opinion
may take and the subject matter, whether fact or opinion, are questions
to be considered.

In examining public opinion, scholars have outlined several
factors as essential for understanding the concept. In the first place,
there is a virtual consensus that public opinion gathers around particular issues. Some early writers especially viewed public opinion as a
semiorganized entity, a collective attitude, personified in simple form
or socialized in more complex structures moving through stages of
deliberation and debate to reach a decision. This organismic view of
the public is inadequate, however. It implies the presence of an issue,
potentially divisive, around which individuals gather. But few issues
attract the attention of an entire population, except perhaps in relatively
small communities where citizen involvement may be widespread and
community consideration may move in conjunction with the mechanisms
of authority to result in a decision by public opinion.[9] Important
aspects, then, of this conception are the extent to which agreement
is widespread, the complexity and range of the issue, and the disposition
of the minor viewpoints. On any one issue opinion need not be unani-
mous; rather, degree of consensus can be considered simply as an
element for study.

But on what types of topics may opinion be considered public?
Perhaps again reflecting an earlier political bias, many American
students of public opinion have limited their regard of public opinion
to a concern with substantive issues of public policy. This focus
excludes an important range of opinion, however. The formation and
reformation of public opinion is not limited to political life; rather,
it pervades all social behavior.[10]

A second factor, one touched upon already, is the nature of the
public involved. At one time it was customary to speak of "the public,"
but it soon became evident that on only a few questions did the entire
citizenry have an opinion. The notion of special publics has been
contrived to describe those segments of the public with views about
particular issues, problems, or questions of specific concern. There
are many such publics, each consisting of individuals who together
are affected by a particular action or idea. It is the issues themselves
that determine the size and character of these publics. Each issue
creates its own public, and this public will not normally consist of the

same individuals who make up any other particular public, although every individual will, at any given time, be a member of many other publics. Thus, the potential for determining "the public" is further undermined, and it becomes clear that clarification of both the issues and the opinions of the publics that form around the issues is essential to a useful discussion of public opinion.

A third major factor in public opinion is the distribution of opinion and the direction, intensity, and stability of individual opinion regarding an issue. Earlier, direction was considered merely in pro-and-con terms, but today it is recognized that this simple polarity often conceals wide gradations in opinion. The number of views that can be differentiated on an issue depends to a large degree upon the attitudes and experiences of the members of the public considered, as well as on the degree of complexity of the issue.

Related to this concept of direction of opinion is the intensity with which an opinion is held. A person may line up anywhere along a scale or continuum measuring the direction of opinion, but he may care a great deal, a little, or scarcely at all about that opinion. Level of intensity may be extremely important, especially in the political sphere, in dictating whether or not an issue receives attention or priority in government affairs.

Degree of stability is another characteristic of public opinion, also affecting the outcome of issues or decisions. Issues that relate to opinions widely held at high stability within a population present radically different problems for government than do those matters on which opinions are unstable or fluid.[11]

It is obvious that the quality of opinion varies considerably. One can distinguish between expert and lay opinion, educated and uninformed opinion, and many other types. One of the problems of public opinion research is assessing these varied characteristics of opinion and deciding whether opinions need be intensely held, stable, rational, or informed to constitute public opinion. It seems clear that these variables affect the influence of opinion, but it is necessary in defining public opinion to avoid becoming confused with evaluating opinion merely on a particular issue or within a special public.

Effectiveness of opinion is another major factor in the definition of public opinion, and perhaps the most important element for analysis. An opinion's degree of influence on individuals, on the society as a whole, or on the governmental process in the political sphere is a function of the number of individuals holding the opinion, the intensity of their feelings, the strenuousness of their effort toward a common objective, and the political and social context in which the opinion operates.[12]

When speaking of the effectiveness of public opinion, an active or participating public is implied. The public is, indeed, a group that participates in the making of public decisions, though the effectiveness of such participation must vary historically and under different social conditions. Public opinion occurs as a function of society in operation and as the result of interaction among diverse views and positions on issues. It implies a decisional conception of the role of the public. Public opinion, then, in this discussion may simply be taken to mean the collective opinion of the electorate or voting public, "those opinions held by individuals which governments find it prudent to heed."[13] Though it is recognized that public opinion need not be limited to the political or governmental sphere, it is useful to the interests here to narrow the conception.

The specific focus here is the relation of mass thinking to the exercise of authority. This focus implies a view of public opinion as "opinions on matters of concern to the nation freely and publicly expressed by men outside the government who claim a right that their opinions should influence or determine the actions, personnel, or structure of their government."[14] What has been suggested so far is that a definition of public opinion is some conception of what constitutes a public and what constitutes an opinion. And the central significance of public opinion is that it participates in the ruling of the community.

Floyd H. Allport's summary, still one of the best, includes among the essential characteristics of public opinion verbalization and communication among many individuals, a widely known issue, and action or readiness for action by individuals who are aware that others are reacting to the same situation, ordinarily a transitory phenomenon.[15] Other scholars have pointed out that public opinion does not necessarily involve a majority, that it must be distinguished from norms and customs, and that its effectiveness in bringing about change depends on the political and social context in which it operates.

Most recently, students of public opinion have focused their attention on the complex process by which opinions are formed. To determine how public opinion is formed is to find out how personal opinions are formed. The public is always a group, a collection of individuals, never an organic entity with an existence of its own. Public opinion is a collection of the opinions of those individuals constituting the public. Personal opinions stem from three basic elements—the person, his environment, and the interaction of the two.[16] The discussion does not require any elaborate examination of this opinion formation process, but it is useful at least to survey the various perspectives on opinion formation as a basis for later comments on the opinion poll.

There is a variety of views among scholars as to the opinion forming process. The simplest and perhaps the most traditional to Western civilization is the rationalist approach, with human reason determining opinion. By the exercise of his reason man is able to understand facts and laws as a basis for his opinions. Several problems apparent in this approach, however, are attested to by the largely non-rational elements involved in some opinions—prejudice, for example. Obviously, reason and intellectual calculation play a role in the opinion forming process but probably are not the sole or most important determinants of public opinion.

Psychology offers another approach to the opinion forming process.[17] The Freudian view in particular suggests that experiences in infancy and early childhood determine the personality structure and attitude patterns of the adult. These characteristics in turn limit and shape not only his self-image but also his social outlook and his view of political issues. His private and public opinions, then, in large part result from the way he perceives and internalizes social events and ideas.

Sociological analysis offers a different approach to the study of opinion formation, relying heavily upon the idea that opinions are shaped by the cultural traditions, social institutions, and group norms of the society of which the individual is a part. Large group and small group factors have been examined for their influence on individual opinion. In more recent research social psychologists have indicated that opinions are strongly influenced both by the network of friends and acquaintances who are seen often or who are important and by the "images" one has of oneself and of the opinions one deems appropriate for oneself.

Various factors have been suggested as essential or at least very important in the opinion forming process. The list includes man's reasoning ability, personality and psychological characteristics, group ties, family, church, school, community, environment, occupation, and the media. It seems clear that the forming of opinions is a function of a complex interaction of many factors, both causal and influential, that are just beginning to be analyzed and explained.

## THE DETERMINATION OF PUBLIC OPINION

If public opinion represents the collective opinions of a number of individuals toward an issue of public importance, results from the complex interaction of man and his environment, and plays a role in legitimizing and controlling democratic and nondemocratic governments, the problem of determining public opinion becomes extremely important. There are a number of indexes of opinion, ranging from the press to the straw poll to the sophisticated sampling techniques that are the core of modern opinion analysis. A brief discussion of the bases for measuring opinions and of the contemporary techniques of opinion polling and their problems will provide a background for the methodology to be used in this section.

That the process of discovering people's opinions involves reading, asking, listening, and thinking is obvious. Newspapers, magazines, television, fan mail—all serve to indicate public reaction toward issues, persons, or candidates. Market research involves almost exclusively the analysis of consumer opinion: why people buy the things they do; what products, services, or programs appeal to the consuming public. In politics the "ear to the ground," the door-to-door canvass, letters to the editor, and straw polls serve to reveal the opinions of constituents or potential voters. Elections and referenda may be considered indexes of public opinion, with voters registering their opinions on issues or candidates directly.

But each of these techniques has its particular problems. Newspapers and the media in general may be isolated from the opinion of readers or listeners; witness the present controversy over the Eastern news establishment. The varied gradations of opinions among the public at large are ignored for purposes of summary and simplification. Consumer research may not detect the inordinate influence of economic conditions apart from the qualities or characteristics of any particular product. Straw polls and other informal devices of political opinion gathering have the problem of obtaining representative groups and are skewed by intensity of feelings and educational level, among other things. To attempt to predict the actions of the many from the stated intentions of the few, or even to generalize on the nature of public sentiment on the basis of the replies of a handful of individuals, is one thing, but to be able to have reasonable confidence in one's conclusions requires, as shall be seen, a more sophisticated methodology than that frequently used by early or amateur poll-takers.[18]

Elections and referenda, especially on a large scale, also have serious problems of accuracy and reliability. They are so cumbersome and expensive that they cannot be used frequently; issues tend to be oversimplified and confused; and the proportion of the voting public actually participating is generally so small that the outcome seldom gives a clear mandate for public policy. Elections may select officials but seldom provide more than a crude index of the electorate's opinion on public issues.

For the most part, these informal devices for determining public opinion provide partial manifestations, not true indications, of public opinion. The basis for modern public opinion polling, however, lies in such efforts as journalistic straw polls, market research, and psychological testing.[19]

Polling the opinions of voters in regard to elections goes back at least as far as the presidential election of 1824, when the Harrisburg Pennsylvanian sought to determine the potential votes of citizens in Wilmington, Delaware. Straw votes were conducted throughout the nineteenth and twentieth centuries, with perhaps the best known being the poll conducted by the Literary Digest between 1916 and 1936. Newspaper publishers discovered and capitalized on widespread public interest in popular opinion about candidates and major issues of public policy. Similarly, the transition to a consumer economy in the early decades of the twentieth century, and the subsequent development of advertising and marketing into an important element of the industrial concern, also contributed much to modern opinion polling. An understanding of testing devices and techniques, human attitudes, motivation, conditioning, and especially probability allowed market researchers to device various methods of sampling to reduce the cost of nationwide consumer surveys. The work of psychologists during World War I with the millions of recruits that required testing also stimulated a growing sophistication in tests and measurements.

The culmination of these several developments was the appearance in the 1930s and early 1940s of several national opinion polls and polling organizations: the American Institute of Public Opinion's Gallup Poll; the Fortune Survey, now the Roper Poll; the Office of Public Opinion Research; the National Opinion Research Center. The publication of the Public Opinion Quarterly and the development of survey centers at universities throughout the nation secured the field of public opinion analysis as a respectable academic interest. Three decades later public opinion polling had spread throughout the world. The World Association for Public Opinion Research had members from 40 countries, and numerous polling organizations were reported to be working in Communist and other countries that were not represented in the Association's membership.[20]

Though the topics and issues explored by polling agencies are as diverse as the issues confronting society, the basic objective of the opinion poll is to assess the feelings and views of a particular group of people who, according to some relevant criteria, are considered representative of the total public, or universe, from which information is desired.[21] The methodology of sampling and statistical analysis of data at times becomes complex, but generally pollsters attempt to follow several distinct steps in the construction and use of a scientific public opinion survey: A statement of purpose or information desired is determined; a relevant universe is chosen; a particular sample size and type is identified; a questionnaire is constructed; interviewers are recruited and trained; the field work is completed; and the responses or data are processed and analyzed.

Each of these steps is essential to the pollster. Each requires further elaboration if one is to consider the variety of methods for determining, for example, the type of sample or the size of sample required for minimum error. The way in which the questionnaire is constructed and ordered, the way in which the interview is conducted in all its aspects, and the way in which the responses are subjected to quantitative and qualitative analysis are all necessary for accuracy and reliability. Here, however, the purposes are limited to describing and recognizing the uses and values of polling and perhaps are better served by a discussion of several of the problems confronting public opinion surveys.

Early poll-takers were misled and confounded by the problem of achieving a representative sample from which to assess opinions and to generalize for a large population. The use of telephone and automobile registrations, supposedly representing the American voting public, as a universe, from which a sample was chosen for the Literary Digest poll, led that magazine to report in advance a large margin of victory for Landon in the 1936 presidential election. The sample greatly overrepresented middle- and upper-income Republicans.[22] Quota sampling, obtaining responses from a sample with characteristics distributed as they are for a universe, was also recognized as inadequate when it was realized that nowhere near all the important factors could be accounted for. Consequently, random or probability sampling was increasingly employed, and the variety of techniques developed since attempt to ensure the representativeness of samples. Another problem confronting pollsters on this same issue is the question of how small a sample can be. Even for a small universe researchers agree that about 200 is a minimum for any useful sample and that samples of less than 50 produce great error.[23]

Errors may occur at every step of the survey process. Questionnaires are difficult to construct if one is to be concise, clear, and free from emotional or biasing characteristics. An interview is greatly affected by a number of factors, including the general attitude and personality of both the interviewer and interviewee and the manner of dress, speech, and tone of the interviewer. The place and time of the encounter can also be reflected in responses. The fact that the interviewer is ordinarily a stranger may very well affect responses, though it is not agreed whether it produces a positive or negative effect.

The competence of the public in responding to questions concerning policy has long been a topic of debate. Aside from distortions of interviewer bias and outright lack of response (the "Don't Know"), there is evidence to indicate that persons polled in opinion surveys tend to overstate their interest, knowledge, and conviction on public questions. As one critic points out, "Public opinion is what you say out loud to anyone. It is an overt and not necessarily candid part of your private opinion."[24] Questions relating opinion and behavior very often reflect heavy social pressure to respond with the respectable answer. It is the degree of correspondence between private opinion and public opinion that interests the psychologist and between public opinion and related behavior that interests the social or political analyst.

Most students of public opinion are willing to agree that the public is more competent to answer some types of questions than others.[25] Sweeping generalizations regarding the competence of public opinion without regard to the type of information sought adds little to understanding. Many attempts have been made to differentiate which questions do or do not lend themselves to public responses. Distinctions have been made between ends and means, with the suggestion that the general public is more capable of determining the ends of public policy than the specific means for attaining those ends. Some have claimed that the average man is better equipped to judge men than measures and parties than issues and that he can better evaluate the results of present policies than new proposals and give vent to grievances than invent remedies. Other distinctions that have been made suggest that the public has greater competence in nontechnical questions than in technical problems, in nonfinancial measures than in financial issues, in specific statutes than in general legislative principles, and in issues within rather than without the everyday experience of people generally. The basic problem, however, is whether there are any types of questions that yield answers from the public so substantively wise and competent that they should influence public policy directly.

The criticisms of the pollsters have not been limited solely to methodological problems. The use of opinion data to imply causal relations, associating opinions with a variety of personal and environmental characteristics, requires care lest the analyst risk overgeneralization or specious correlation. No matter how much quantitative analysis one is able to do with poll data, the evidence is rarely clearcut and neatly stacked for or against hypotheses. Opinions of different publics can be compared in great detail, although some information may be lost in standardizing data. The possibilities for comparisons and correlations seem to be virtually unlimited, however, and the probing for new and more significant aspects is a most promising, if timeless, task.

The use of opinion data has also been attacked. Some critics suggest that mass opinion data is worthless because it fails to account for the relative competence of individual opinions and the likelihood that it represents the views of persons incapable of making their views effective.[26] The effects of polls on leadership, elections, and representative government have been decried. Bandwagon effects, an inordinate influence on candidate choice, an obeisance to public opinion on the part of legislators and executives alike—all are counted among the adverse results of opinion polls. One noted critic, Walter Lippmann, assails pollsters and officials for enthroning public opinion and letting it have the upper hand in the policy-making process.[27]

Pollsters, probably more than other people, appreciate the difficulties they face. They are aware of the possibilities for error and, when they can resist economic and journalistic pressures, recognize that they have no magical tools to reflect accurately each movement of public opinion. Their consensus, however, is that the polls do serve worthwhile purposes. The impact of public opinion on government, the role of the polls in checking inflated claims of candidates and pressure groups, and the expanding use of public opinion surveys in many areas too numerous to mention reflect for the pollsters a growing acceptance of and satisfaction with the polls on the part of the public. The public opinion survey presents a useful tool to the social scientist if careful scrutiny and attention is applied. Each public opinion survey must be judged on its own merits, and even if every precaution is taken the results must be considered not as scientific truth but with a certain degree of skeptical confidence and an appreciation of how difficult it is to measure, much less to interpret, public opinion scientifically.

**PUBLIC OPINION
IN A DEMOCRACY**

The historical evolution of the concept of public opinion has been noted, its varied characteristics examined, and the problems of its measurement discussed. The importance of the link between decision-making and public opinion has always been recognized. Over several centuries the right to govern came to be located in the consent of the governed. And the ideas, beliefs, and symbols associated with this democratic ideology have such a powerful and universal appeal that even modern dictatorships have taken over much of the symbolism and semantics of democracy.[1] Yet to define the role of public opinion as it influences particular policies in different situations presents a difficult analytical problem.

Earlier approaches to this problem were limited by the lack of empirical data relating to the link between public opinion and governmental policy. Writers were quick to reaffirm their belief that opinion should and did influence public policy. "It is . . . on opinion only that government is founded; and this maxim extends to the most despotic and most military governments, as well as to the most free and most popular."[2] Even critics of public opinion, who, along with Lippmann, assert that public opinion has altogether too much influence and that it is largely responsible for the mistakes of policy-makers in the past,[3] assume that some relation exists between opinion and government. The debate over whether or not public opinion should influence public policy continues. The interest here and in the next section is to attempt to determine to what extent, if at all, public opinion actually influences public policy.

The focus is limited in that the link between opinion and policy in a democratic state, specifically at the local government level, is being explored. Yet these efforts may be important to the understanding of the role of public opinion in any society, for, as suggested, all governments must concern themselves with public opinion. They

cannot maintain authority by force alone. Rather, they must seek
willing acceptance and conformity from most of their citizens.[4]

The opinion-policy process denotes the relationship of what
people think to what government does.[5] In democratic societies
government is by the people: what the people want ought to be exactly
what the government does. The obvious model for this straightforward
process is the New England town, the small, self-contained community,
where deliberation and decision on town issues takes place en masse
in a town meeting. But this simple model misses much. How often
do citizens meet? Do they handle even the most minute questions?
What happens to minority opinion? The traditional view of the place
of public opinion in a democracy suffers from several serious faults.
It tends to ignore both custom and emotion; it assumes faultless
social communication; and it demands what Walter Lippmann calls
the "omnicompetent citizen" (that is, it ignores specialization of
function). It is probably not applicable, in anything like its ideal
form, to a modern, industrialized, urbanized, and specialized society.[6]

If one rules out the notion of the people governing themselves,
and one student of public opinion insists that opinion as a process
operating within the public is by definition to be distinguished from
governing,[7] then the focus of attention is placed on the formal and
informal means of public participation in governmental affairs.
Viewing democracy as a method of decision-making rather than as
a form of government involving direct citizen rule requires that one
examine all potential political linkages, whether direct or indirect.
A linkage between the public and its government is the mechanism
that allows leaders to act in accordance with the wants, needs, and
demands of their public.[8] Several such mechanisms have been
suggested, such as elections, political parties, pressure groups, and
public opinion polls. Exploring the nature of these linkages enables
one to examine some fundamental questions of governmental effectiveness, public opinion, and democracy.

The basic concern here is with the relationship between democracy and public policy. There is a group of political theorists who
very clearly see no place for the democratic process in the formation
of public policy. Theorists such as Gaetano Mosca, Vilfredo Pareto,
and Roberto Michels suggest a deterministic inevitability that oligar-
chies will develop to rule organizations of any type and dimension;
they prescribe this type of rule as the only one that will ensure the
successful operation of the system. Disagreement exists, however,
among U.S. analysts, who possess the value orientation that democracy
should be the credo of the nation, yet who recognize that the democratic process does not pervade the environment in which public policy is
made. Some form of linkage between public opinion and policy formation would have to be demonstrated before one could call the public
policy process a democratic one.

Some analysts have argued that there are linkages among public opinion, voting, and public policy but that these connections are very indirect and subtle. V. O. Key feels that, while public opinion often cannot directly control public policy, it does produce a system of "dikes" that place certain parameters on public action and set a range of discretion within which government may act or within which debate at official levels may proceed.[9] The results of a number of survey analyses of the U.S. voter are less optimistic about the existence of democratic controls on the government. These studies, in general terms, find an overwhelming amount of determinism in U.S. voting and do not see voting as a process for controlling public policy formation by a rational analysis of politicians' policy pronouncements.[10]

Other attempts, using the case study method, have sought to discover the relationship between public opinion and specific public policy decisions. Conclusions from several of these studies reveal the following:[11]

1. The relationship between public opinion and public policy varies greatly from issue to issue. Influence may be direct or indirect, may be exerted quickly or slowly, and may change over time or remain constant.

2. The extent of the influence of public opinion on public policy is dependent on a variety of factors, including the degree of unanimity, the intensity of opinions, the clarity of the issues, and the nature and extent of organized support for and against the public position.

3. Some obstacles to the easy translation of public opinion into public policy include the difficulty of determining public opinion on a specific issue in a form useful to policy-makers but within the competence of the public, special groups and interests that attempt to make their voices appear to be the majority, and a filtering through more or less representative legislative and administrative bodies with built-in rules and procedures that check the free, effective flow of public opinion.

4. The nature of the influence of opinion on policy includes the limiting of governmental decisions because a rather widespread knowledge of its tolerances dampen leadership, with officials generally reluctant to take a stand in the face of probable widespread popular disapproval. Public opinion seldom acts positively to promote a new policy but often acts negatively to demonstrate its dissatisfaction with existing policies; it may be a powerful instrument of control, but after rather than before the fact.

5. The relationship between opinion and policy is two-way, cyclical, and dynamic; opinion influences policy and policy influences opinion. As general policies become more specific, their implications may be better understood, and opinion may change.

6. The relationship is also affected by a variety of other factors, including government itself, through information, propaganda, official actions, the mass media, private interest group propaganda, and even significant events.

Scholars have also attempted to discover the role of public opinion in government through the formulation of theoretical models. Within the literature of political science numerous models have attempted to describe the democratic nature of public policy formation. Probably the simplest approach is what has come to be called the "rational-activist" model.[12] According to this conceptualization, the individual citizen must be able to gather and comprehend all relevant political information and be able to make rational calculations as to how he individually is affected by the information he has gathered. He is then expected to calculate carefully which of the various candidate's positions best reflect his own personal preferences and then to vote for that candidate. Hence, if an elected official or candidate neglects the demands of the majority, voters will recognize his omission and deny him support in future elections. The most obvious problem with this model is that it would provide the basis for a democratic policy process only if all members of the particular system demonstrated this rational calculation. If a substantial proportion of people demonstrate more deterministic voting patterns, however, they cannot be regarded as rationally influencing the policy process through their vote.

A second approach that attempts to show the democratic nature of public policy formation is the political parties model.[13] This model requires the same kind of reasoning calculation as the rational-activist model but saves the individual from having to consider every candidate by allowing him merely to consider which party's program best reflects his preferences. In order to retain its credibility in the future, the party must see that all the elected officials who use its banner conform to its platform. The individual can then assess the performance of the party in control of government and, if dissatisfied, deny it his vote in the future. This model suffers the same malaise as the rational-activist model in that all individuals do not demonstrate this rationality, despite the economy in consideration of candidates that party identification provides. The party model contains a further difficulty in that parties have not demonstrated the ability to enforce conformity from their elected officials, thus further compromising the suggestion that the people retain democratic control over policy by voting for the party of their choice.

A third approach can be called the group model.[14] This model suggests that the individual is relatively impotent in modern society and that groups instead are the source of all effective opinion. Thus, by definition this model shifts the necessity to show a linkage between public policy and public opinion to the need to demonstrate a linkage between policy and group opinion. Despite the economy of having to deal with a much smaller number of actors, in that there are fewer groups than individuals, this model has its own profound problems. First, groups vary in the magnitude of their influence, and influence level does not always correlate with group size. Thus, even if certain groups did control policy formation, these groups might still represent only a small minority of the population. Second, even if a correlation between group influence and size did exist, the complication of people having multimemberships in conflicting groups would threaten the credibility of the model.

A fourth approach is the "sharing" model.[15] This model suggests that to some degree leaders give expression to public demands merely because they share preferences with the public. The implication is that political leaders are a representative sample of the public. Hence, leaders' preferences in public policy are a fair approximation of the people's preferences. Furthermore, since democratic procedures regulate political conflict and protect the privileged position of leaders in the system, these leaders can be counted on to defend the democratic creed and thus to respond to their public's wishes.[16] The problem with this model is that, unlike the three earlier ones, it does not even pretend to have any coercive power; thus, no correction is possible when leaders do not share their public's attitudes, even if those attitudes are accurately discernible.

A final approach might be called the "role-playing" model.[17] This model suggests that a linkage between policy and the public may exist in that the political leader sees his role as that of spokesman for the preferences, desires, and demands of his constituency. Clearly, as in the belief-sharing model, the people possess no coercive power over the leader and have no recourse when the leader stops seeing himself as their spokesman. In addition, this model assumes that the leader can somehow discern the preferences of the majority.

Probably no single model adequately describes the complex matrix of action and interaction that has been termed the opinion-policy process. Each model focuses upon certain aspects of the linkage between opinion and policy-making and may therefore be useful. The process is not one of translating a single popular will into public policy. In fact, the essence of democratic government may rest not in any mirroring of opinion by government but in the government's concern in good faith for public preferences and in its dedication to mass interests: "A complex interaction occurs, with government (and other centers of influence as well) affecting the form and content of opinion; and, in turn, public opinion may condition the manner, content, and timing of public action."[18]

Why is public opinion important in American government?
First, the general bounds of public policy are set by latent public
attitudes. For instance, in the United States the nationalization of
industry or government control of the press is precluded by underlying
public attitudes. Such limitations operate also in nondemocratic systems.
The government of the Soviet Union, for instance, embarked on a
campaign against religion that later had to be modified because it
was difficult to enforce and destroyed the people's morale. Today the
Soviet government has elaborate and expensive procedures for keeping
in touch with public opinion to prevent similar debacles.[19]

Elected officials in the democratic system acquire knowledge
of public opinion through a free press and periodic elections, a second
reason for the importance of public opinion. On election day the broad
preferences and goals of public policy are expressed by the public.
Although election results carry no clear mandate for those elected
with respect to a specific policy area, it is not uncommon for elected
officials to act as if they had a mandate. In this way elections are
considered very general expressions of public opinion, at least of
the opinion of that segment of the population that votes.

Third, public opinion can play a supportive or legitimizing
function for specific public policy areas. For instance, the Social
Security Act of 1935 was bitterly opposed by Republicans, but public
opinion has come to endorse the program to the point that Barry
Goldwater recommended an extension of the system in his 1964
campaign for the presidency. In short, the building of favorable
public opinion over time can give a program agreement or substantial
support and thereby legitimize the acts of the original decision-makers.

Finally, public opinion serves a demand function. Women's
suffrage, medical care for the aged, voting rights for Negroes,
assistance for the poor—all are examples of the public expression of
demands and their ultimate reflection in policy. Opinions on public
issues need not always be identical with political demands, but public
opinion may finally be quite influential in stimulating and shaping
demands.[20]


## METHODOLOGY

In searching for empirical evidence concerning the role played
by public opinion in the policy-making process, an attempt was made
to determine the opinions of a sample of the voting age population in
one metropolitan area, Onondaga County, New York. Specifically,
the concern was with the opinions of citizens as to the ordering of
priorities in the metropolitan area. The setting of priorities for
the city, increasingly important because of the scarcity of resources,

the fragmentation and decentralization of local governments, and the larger role played by state and federal governments, is an attempt to bring some order to the complexity of the urban polity. The intention was to know what the public felt about metropolitan priorities because their opinions are fundamental to the argument behind the maintenance of any governmental system that claims to be democratic.

The hypothesis here was rather straightforward: Public priority preferences vary widely on the basis of social, economic, and demographic circumstances. Consequently, any authoritative ordering of metropolitan areawide public priorities will advantage certain publics and disadvantage others. This problem is deceptively simple. The setting of priorities, and the allocation of scarce resources in accord with those priorities, is not a normatively neutral activity.[21] Still, there is a paucity of evidence as to who is being advantaged or disadvantaged by a particular pattern of public priorities. Furthermore, and probably more important, little is known about which particular publics feel more or less advantaged by specific urban priorities. Thus, although one may in a general sense be aware that certain sets of priorities serve particular interests, there is little substantive knowledge of how they do so.

It is contended here that knowledge of public priorities can be expanded by the use of general survey techniques. This is accomplished, initially, by determining how the people feel about priorities—a rather fundamental step in a system claiming to be democratic. Then these attitudes are contrasted with real urban priorities, measured by public spending. In this way, there is an attempt to assess which groups are being advantaged and which ones disadvantaged by the present pattern of public priorities. While this measurement reveals little about the nature of the policy-making process, the topic of a later chapter, it does indicate success or achievement in the policy process through use of outputs or end products.

A stratified random sample was taken of the population of the Syracuse standard metropolitan statistical (SMSA) area in the late summer of 1967. In the city and its contiguous suburbs a grid technique was used to divide the area into numbered sections. Grid numbers were then selected randomly, as were ten residences within each section. If possible, a voting-age person was interviewed at each residence.

Fifty-seven percent of the respondents were female, lending the sample a slight female bias. Forty-six percent of the sample lived in the central city, while the remainder lived in the suburbs and rural areas, a close approximation of the urban/rural ratio for Onondaga County (47% in Syracuse City) as set out in a special 1966 New York State Census of Population.[22] The sample is regarded as representative of the universe at the 0.05 level of confidence, using the standard error of mean test.

## CONCEPTIONS REGARDING THE
## IMPORTANCE OF URBAN PROBLEMS

An open selection technique was used to assess each respondent's set of urban priority preferences. The question was as follows:

> There are many problems which we face locally—in this city and county. Of those listed below, which do you believe are the most important? Beside all those problems which you consider most important, write a "1". (The interviewer actually did the writing). Write a "2" beside those you consider somewhat less important. Write a "3" beside those you consider least important.

| | |
|---|---|
| _____Education | _____Police Protection |
| _____Welfare | _____Maintenance of Streets |
| _____Water Pollution | _____Adequate Water |
| _____Employment | _____Traffic Tie-ups |
| _____Housing | _____Parks and Recreational Facilities |

By using the free selection technique, no respondent was forced to make precise one-to-ten rankings of the importance of each function. It was desired to know how great a distinction citizens make regarding the relative importance of different urban problems. The free selection approach allowed the respondents to consider every problem most important, or none important, so this technique did not presume that everyone regarded at least some urban problems as important.

When all 1,036 persons in the sample are taken together, their urban priority preferences are as shown in Table 11.

Finding education and police protection as first- and second-level priorities is little surprise. But finding water pollution ahead of employment, welfare, street maintenance, housing, traffic, and park and recreation facilities is most interesting. This trend may indicate that strong feelings are developing about the need for water pollution abatement generally and that it is widely held to be the third-order urban priority. It may be, however, that Onondaga County is somewhat unique with respect to this particular problem. In the center of the highly populated portion of the county is Onondaga Lake, a small body of water roughly two miles wide and four miles long. Onondaga Lake is highly polluted with both industrial and city wastes and as a result is unsightly, odorous, and unusable. This condition is a regular theme in both the local press and political campaigns.

In addition, there has been a local radio and television anti-water-pollution campaign financed by the national government. As a consequence, the priority given to water pollution by the residents of Onondaga County may be in part a reflection of a particular local problem. On the other hand, the residents of New York State passed $1 billion water pollution bond issue in 1966 by a majority of three to one, clearly an indication of the importance they attach to the problem and their willingness to spend in order to deal with it.

The three urban problems that represent rather direct human needs all fall in the range of middle-level priorities. Employment is fourth, welfare sixth, and housing eighth. This level of priority is probably due to the fact that these three problems are not generally regarded as primarily public in the same way that education and police protection are. Of the three welfare and housing have a more public character than employment, so it is somewhat surprising that 52 percent of the respondents consider employment a most important problem, whereas only 41 and 39 percent, respectively, regard welfare and housing as most important. This indication may suggest that substantial percentages of the county do not feel secure in their employment and regard this not just as a personal problem but as a public question.

Like most other SMSAs, Syracuse has a traffic problem, coupled with serious difficulties in street maintenance. Yet these two problems are well down the list of priorities. It is necessary to note, however, that while only 26 percent of our respondents regarded traffic as a

TABLE 11

Respondents' Priority Preferences

| Problem | Percent Considering Most Important |
|---|---|
| Education | 81 |
| Police protection | 70 |
| Water pollution | 56 |
| Employment | 52 |
| Adequate water | 42 |
| Welfare | 41 |
| Maintenance of streets | 40 |
| Housing | 39 |
| Traffic tie-ups | 26 |
| Park and recreational facilities | 25 |

most serious problem, almost double that amount (40 percent) consider
street maintenance most important. Still, in view of all respondents
taken together, traffic and street maintenance are distinctly less
important than education, police protection, water pollution, employment, water adequacy, and welfare.

## The Urban-Suburban Contrast

To understand more fully urban priorities, one must disaggre-
gate them, or break them down. The first step is on the basis of
place of residence, where one finds the following differences in
priority preferences (see Table 12).

Here one can see some rather fundamental differences. The
most salient is seen in the urban residents' priority preference for
direct needs, particularly employment and housing, which they rank
third and fourth. Suburban residents regard them as fourth and
eighth-level preferences. And, as city respondents rank welfare
seventh and suburbanites rank it sixth, 45 percent of the former
regard it as most important, as against only 35 percent of the latter.
From this breakdown it appears that suburban residents are more
secure in their housing, employment, and welfare and are therefore
more concerned about less basic matters, such as water pollution,
which they rank third, and adequate water, which they rank fifth. To
the city residents these are priorities of only the fifth and eighth
orders. City and suburban residents, then, agree that education is
most important, followed by law enforcement. After that, however,
city residents tend to be more concerned with direct human needs,
such as employment, housing, and welfare, whereas suburbanites
consider water adequacy and pollution more important.

## The Income Differential

When urban priority preferences are broken down on the basis
of the annual income level of the family of the respondent, the pattern
in Table 13 emerges. Most notable in this array is the tendency of
people from families with annual incomes less than $7,000 to regard
many more of the urban problems as most important. A possible explanation is that people from lower income families are probably from
a generally lower socioeconomic status. Therefore, they tend to regard
many things as most important. Second, persons from lower income
families may consider many more of these problems to be public, wherea
those from higher income families are able to supply certain of these

TABLE 12

Respondents' Priority Preferences,
by Place of Residence

| Urban | | Suburban | |
|---|---|---|---|
| Problem | Percent Considering Most Important | Problem | Percent Considering Most Important |
| Education | 78 | Education | 82 |
| Police protection | 68 | Police protection | 70 |
| Employment | 54 | Water pollution | 60 |
| Housing | 50 | Employment | 49 |
| Street maintenance | 46 | Welfare | 35 |
| Welfare | 45 | Street maintenance | 32 |
| Adequate water | 32 | Housing | 24 |
| Park and recreational facilities | 28 | Traffic tie-ups | 24 |
| Traffic tie-ups | 26 | Park and recreational facilities | 20 |

needs privately and thus attach less importance to such things as public park and recreation facilities and housing.

Again, one can see that education and police protection are the first- and second-order priorities, respectively, of both income groups. There is an important distinction, however; those in the lower income category attach more importance to police protection than do those in the higher income group (74 percent to 61 percent). This is probably evidence that it is those in low income categories rather than those in high income groups that feel most threatened by crime, perhaps because of its proximity and because they would feel a loss more severely.

As was evident in contrasting the responses of city and suburban residents, there is a difference based on income level in the priorities attached to water pollution and employment. Pollution control is more important to those in the higher income category and the suburbanites, whereas employment is more important to lower income and city residents.

TABLE 13

Respondents' Priority Preferences,
by Income Level

| Income Under $7,000 | | Income over $7,000 | |
| --- | --- | --- | --- |
| Problem | Percent Considering Most Important | Problem | Percent Considering Most Important |
| Education | 81 | Education | 80 |
| Police protection | 74 | Police protection | 61 |
| Employment | 58 | Water pollution | 59 |
| Water pollution | 53 | Employment | 42 |
| Street maintenance | 52 | Welfare | 39 |
| Housing | 48 | Adequate water | 38 |
| Adequate water | 47 | Street maintenance | 29 |
| Welfare | 46 | Housing | 28 |
| Traffic tie-ups | 33 | Traffic tie-ups | 20 |
| Park and recreational facilities | 31 | Park and recreational facilities | 19 |

There are other differences in priorities based on differences in family income level, but they tend to cancel each other out. For instance, welfare is the eighth-order priority for those below $7,000, whereas it is the fifth-order priority for those above $7,000. By looking at the percentages, however, one can see that more (46 percent) in the lower income category regard welfare as most important than do those in the upper income category (39 percent). This cancelling effect is largely the result of the previously described tendency for those in the lower income group to regard many local functions as most important, having greater difficulty than those in the higher income groups in ordering priorities.

The Educational Contrast

When the respondents are contrasted on the basis of education, the results resemble approximately the variations found on the basis of income differences. This similarity is to be expected because income level is in good part a reflection of educational achievement.

TABLE 14

Respondents' Priority Preferences,
by Education Level

| Up to and Including High School | | Some College | |
|---|---|---|---|
| Problem | Percent Considering Most Important | Problem | Percent Considering Most Important |
| Education | 82 | Education | 79 |
| Police protection | 75 | Police protection | 63 |
| Employment | 62 | Water pollution | 58 |
| Water pollution | 55 | Welfare | 42 |
| Adequate water | 52 | Employment | 41 |
| Street main- | | Adequate water | 35 |
| tenance | 47 | Housing | 31 |
| Housing | 45 | Street main- | |
| Welfare | 37 | tenance | 30 |
| Traffic tie-ups | 31 | Traffic tie-ups | 21 |
| Park and rec- | | Park and rec- | |
| reational | | reational | |
| facilities | 27 | facilities | 21 |

Again, one can see those with less education being more concerned about police protection and ranking employment well above water pollution, while those with more education indicate priorities in the reverse order. (See Table 14.) Here, however, the differences are more stark. Those with less education consider employment more important (62 percent), whereas of those with more education only 41 percent consider it so. As was found in the contrasts by income, those with lower education have a tendency to regard many more local functions to be most important and to have a rather low capacity for the distinct ordering of priorities.

The importance attached to the welfare function is perhaps the most interesting aspect of the division on the basis of educational level. Those with less education place it eighth, with 37 percent, whereas those with greater education rank it fourth, with 42 percent. This pattern is doubtless a reflection of the general political science finding that those with lower socioeconomic status have a tendency to have conservative views even of those kinds of government programs from which they are most likely to benefit and for which they are least likely to pay.

### Age and Sex Contrasts

When urban priorities are contrasted on the basis of age, little variation is found. Age differences are as shown in Table 15. Older persons appear to be slightly more concerned about police protection, water pollution, and street maintenance than are younger persons, but these differences are negligible.

The difference between male and female urban priority preferences are not great, as Table 16 shows. There is a very slight tendency for females to regard more local problems as more important, but otherwise there is little difference in priority preference on the basis of sex.

### Generalizations

To generalize on the basis of these findings, it is safe to conclude, first, that these respondents clearly regard education and police protection as the first- and second-order urban priority preferences and that differences in age, sex, income, place of residence, and education have little influence on this pattern. The only exception to this generalization is that older, less educated, and lower income persons tend to have stronger preferences for police protection than do their counterparts. Second, it appears that the level of family income, the place of residence, and the level of education influence priority preferences in the middle range. Less educated persons, less well-off persons, and persons living in the central city tend to regard more direct human needs such as employment and housing as higher priorities, whereas their counterparts consider less basic problems such as water pollution and water adequacy as more important. This evidence seems rather straightforward in indicating that middle-level priorities do differ on the basis of variations in income, education, and place of residence and that generalizations about the set of urban priority preferences are unwarranted. Beyond the agreement on education and law enforcement there are clearly different sets of urban priority preferences based on socioeconomic status. Finally, it appears that age and sex have little influence on urban priorities.

### Real Priorities

The actual or real priorities of the collective governments of Onondaga County are best indicated by the pattern of their expenditures. (See Table 17.) The importance that decision-makers in each county

TABLE 15

Respondents' Priority Preferences, by Age

| Up to 40 | | 40 and over | |
| --- | --- | --- | --- |
| Problem | Percent Considering Most Important | Problem | Percent Considering Most Important |
| Education | 81 | Education | 82 |
| Police protection | 67 | Police protection | 72 |
| Water pollution | 55 | Water pollution | 56 |
| Employment | 50 | Employment | 53 |
| Welfare | 40 | Adequate water | 44 |
| Street main- | | Welfare | 42 |
| tenance | 38 | Housing | 41 |
| Adequate water | 38 | Street main- | |
| Housing | 36 | tenance | 40 |
| Traffic tie-ups | 27 | Park and rec- | |
| Park and rec- | | reational | |
| reational | | facilities | 27 |
| facilities | 22 | Traffic tie-ups | 26 |

department attach to each local government function is a true reflection of their priority preferences, but these indications may not match those determined by the survey. By contrasting spending priorities with the various public priorities, one can determine which particular public is having its priorities best met. This comparison must be made with some caution, however, for some functions of local government are inherently more costly than others. Education, for instance, is a local service that requires extensive capital facilities, large staffs, and great quantities of materials and supplies. By contrast, park and recreation facilities are less costly to build, to staff, and to supply. Comparing the percent of total county spending for each function must, therefore, be interpreted in light of these differences. To aid this comparison, percent figures are provided for three different years—1957, 1962, and 1967—to allow for a modest gauge as to the direction in which real priorities moved during the ten-year period.

There is a second problem in comparing the survey results with spending priorities. When a respondent to the survey indicates

TABLE 16

Respondents' Priority Preferences, by Sex

| Male | | Female | |
|---|---|---|---|
| Problem | Percent Considering Most Important | Problem | Percent Considering Most Important |
| Education | 81 | Education | 82 |
| Police protection | 67 | Police protection | 72 |
| Water pollution | 55 | Water pollution | 56 |
| Employment | 50 | Employment | 53 |
| Welfare | 40 | Adequate water | 44 |
| Street maintenance | 38 | Welfare | 42 |
| Adequate water | 38 | Housing | 41 |
| Housing | 27 | Street maintenance | 40 |
| Traffic tie-ups | 27 | Park and recreational facilities | 27 |
| Park and recreational facilities | 22 | Traffic tie-ups | 26 |

that he regards welfare, for example, as most important, it does not necessarily mean that he feels more should be spent on welfare, and it may mean the opposite. The local problems a respondent considers most important might not be the ones on which he feels the most money should be spent, although it is probably safe to say that there is a rather close association.

Education received the highest proportion of public spending in the county, and there was a sharp increase between 1957 and 1962, matching its priority position as reflected in the survey. Police protection spending is well down the list of expenditure categories but is the number two priority in the judgment of the respondents. There is little doubt that law enforcement activities are by their nature less costly than other functions, which doubtless accounts for its position among spending categories. Still, police spending as a percent of total spending declined from 1957 to 1967. This drop might be interpreted as moving in a direction opposite the importance attached to this function by the respondents.

TABLE 17

Public Spending in Onondaga
County, Selected Years[a]
(in percent)

| Function | 1957 | 1962 | 1967[b] |
|---|---|---|---|
| Education | 36 | 44 | 45 |
| Welfare | 11 | 10 | 13 |
| Streets | 14 | 9 | 9 |
| Housing (includes urban renewal) | – | 6 | 8 |
| Water supply | 5 | 5 | 4 |
| Police protection | 5 | 3 | 3 |
| Sanitation (sewage only) | 6 | 3 | 3 |
| Park and recreational facilities | 3 | 2 | 2 |

[a]Certain of the problems are not reflected in these spending categories. Water pollution abatement, for instance, is only partially reflected by sanitation spending. No figures are available for traffic control or employment spending. The latter is a state level function.

[b]The 1967 spending data were gathered by mail and telephone from the several jurisdictions in the Syracuse SMSA.

Source: U.S. Bureau of the Census, 1957 and 1962 Census of Governments, Government in New York, VI, No. 30 (1957), and VII, No. 32 (1962).

Welfare and housing are second- and fourth-order expenditure categories but tend to be lower order priorities in the survey results. These results also indicate that welfare and housing are regarded as more important by less well-educated, lower income respondents. The status of these functions in the real spending priorities of the jurisdictions in the county seems to indicate that there is some public response to the needs and demands of this group of residents. Because less well-educated and lower income residents are likely to pay less and receive more for these services, it is probably fair to conclude that it is this group that is being primarily advantaged by the rather high status of these functions in real spending priorities. Still, both housing and welfare services are very costly in terms of the number of persons or families aided per dollar of public spending. Therefore, although welfare and housing are rather high spending priorities, these services may be making only a modest impact on the quality of living of those with little education and income.

Water pollution control tends to be a middle- to upper-level priority in the findings, while sanitation spending (sewerage only) is rather well down the expenditure list and declined between 1957 and 1967. On the other hand, the overwhelming passage of the New York State Pure Waters Act in 1965, accompanied by a bond issue of $1 billion, is rather direct evidence of the importance of this issue in the state. Major spending under this program is just beginning and is, therefore, not reflected in the spending priorities listed here. The passage of the bond issue and the general observation that water and air pollution are basic middle-class issues match the general argument here that water pollution control is a more important priority to those with higher incomes and more education, who are more likely to live in the suburbs. Major public spending for water pollution control in the greater Syracuse area would more particularly meet the interests of middle- and upper-level socioeconomic groups than the interests of the lower socioeconomic class, which is basically concerned with the more fundamental needs of housing and employment.

On the basis of this comparison it is fair to say that public priorities attached to education are being met by the proportion of total spending received by that function. It appears that central city residents, persons with lower education and lower incomes, are receiving moderate preferences in the welfare and housing spending categories. Conversely, suburbanites and higher income and education publics are not receiving their preferences for water pollution control and water supply as directly. All groups, but notably central city and lower income and education persons, indicate strong priorities for law enforcement spending, yet spending for this function is well down the list. This fact may indicate popular support for increased police spending or may mean general interest in police deployment and methods.

Street maintenance and traffic control tend to be middle- to low-range public priorities, yet street spending is third in the expenditure rankings. This spending, however, includes some street construction as well as maintenance costs. The rather low relative importance attached to street maintenance by the respondents may be an indication that they regard this need as generally well met.

The argument, based on these findings, that middle and upper socioeconomic groups have a different order of public priorities than their lower socioeconomic counterparts, can be interpreted as disagreeing with the conclusions of some voting studies.[23] On the basis of these studies it is generally held that suburban, better-educated, and higher income persons are more likely to vote for bond issues that are designed to aid the entire community. The conclusion is that higher socioeconomic status is associated with a greater sense of community commitment, even to programs designed to aid primarily lower socioeconomic groups. Higher status groups will give greater support to bond issues that are designed to aid the entire community, particularly the economically disadvantaged, but if they are polled as to which government programs they regard as most salient they give greater priority to those programs that are more directly aligned to their interests, such as water pollution control and water supply. Furthermore, although lower socioeconomic groups tend to have more conservative voting patterns on bond issues from which they are more likely to benefit, their general set of government priorities tends to their fundamental interests in housing and employment. This generalization, of course, is limited to Syracuse and defers to the conclusion that there is basic agreement on the primacy of education and law enforcement.

As urban population continues to grow and urban living to become more complex, the question of public priorities will increase in importance. It will no doubt continue to receive widespread consideration in the popular press and political rhetoric. Continued empirical research of the priorities question can be a vital aid to decision-makers generally and to students of urban government particularly. Research projects similar to the one described herein could tell one the extent to which Onondaga County is representative of SMSAs generally and to what degree it is unique. Furthermore, and more important, such research results should indicate the degree of congruence between publicly held urban priorities and real priorities as they are represented by the pattern of urban public financial investments.

# 6

## THE
## POLICY-MAKING
## PROCESS

Studies of political life have concentrated on such facets as order, power, the state, decision-making, and the monopolization of the use of legitimate force.[1] The overall purpose of the political process, however, is the making of public policy. The policy-making process is not one of the standard fields of political science nor is it one of the traditional fields of inquiry in the history of political thought. But its recent emphasis reflects a growing curiosity on the part of social scientists. Decision-making, or the policy process, the process through which political decisions on public policies are made, has come to be the most generalized new concept in political research.[2]

The study of public policy is a focus that lends itself to many analytical purposes, such as identifying crucial lines of influence in the policy process through theoretical frameworks; measuring and analyzing outputs or policies; discovering various determinants of the policy process, such as social and economic features, political behavior, and governmental structure; studying elections and the role of the voter in the choice of policy-makers; determining types of political socialization; and evaluating economic development.[3] No effort is made here to develop a general theory of the policy process. Rather the authors wish to identify some of the aspects of the process and to analyze some of the forces that shape policy in four functional areas: law enforcement, social services, education, and water pollution control.

The survey of the attitudes of the residents of the metropolitan area will serve as a backdrop to this phase of the report of the results of this study. Up to this point these attitudes have been discussed, expenditures of the local government analyzed, and assessments made of the nature of influence relations between local, state, and federal decision-makers in the four substantive areas of government isolated for the study. In this section these variables shall be related to the policy-making process itself.

The policy-making process is complex and disorderly; it is continuous, with no clear-cut beginning and no end; and it is seldom, if ever, bound to the institutional configurations of the system of government. Thus, an examination of the policy process involves not only analysis of the institutions and structures of society but also exploration of those processes and patterns of interaction that are common to and cut across structural boundaries. [4] The necessity of examining political life in a dynamic context was suggested earlier. The concepts of power and community were analyzed in processual terms: Power was referred to as a flow of interchange, communication, interaction, and influence, measured by the extent to which a person or organization can act out its character; community was referred to as a social configuration with increasing differentiation of function and structure and a growing orientation toward vertical interests and associations. The analysis of the distribution of power at the local level revealed that influence is not concentrated but rather shared among institutions, actors, and levels of government.

The concept of public opinion was viewed in a similar context, with focus on the public opinion process, the formation and reformation of opinions on public issues, and the role of opinion in the policy process, a role described as indirect and dynamic, constantly changing in direction and intensity. No simple model sufficed in describing the interaction of public opinion and public policy in a complex mesh of obstacles and concerns.

In discussing the policy-making process one is tempted to suggest that policy is made through a series of steps, regular and recurring sequences of behavior. Some of the patterns that have been identified include the following:[5]

> formation—the indication or articulation of a need in public terms;
> articulation—the presentation of issues in the public arena with a variety of methods and strategies;
> mobilization—the securing of allies and neutralizing of enemies;
> codification—the process of bargaining and debate leading to a decision;
> application—the implementation of a decision to a specific case; and
> redefinition—the interaction of feedback and influence to produce revision.

This way of looking at policy-making is useful for some purposes but tends to oversimplify the process. Policy-making is continuous and dynamic, and such distinctions of stages are artificial. Temporal categories overlap. The ways in which problems are articulated affect the ways in which issues are defined, which in turn affect the solutions and the institutions from which recourse is sought.[6] Somehow, a complex set of forces all taken together as policy-making produces effects called policies.

This system of interaction that is called the policy process involves all institutions and levels of government. It is in examining the roles of participants in the policy-making system that the dynamic character of this process is revealed. If the study of politics is concerned with understanding how authoritative decisions are made and executed for society, then one must concern oneself with that system of social interaction on the part of individuals and groups that translates private needs into collective community action.[7] The following pages present an attempt to explore the processual nature of political interactions.

## POWER AND THE POLICY-MAKING PROCESS

Important sources (and, as shall be indicated later, perhaps the most important sources in the long run) of public policy are found within a program context, involving an organized, special-purpose institution with an essentially cyclical life process, with repetitive patterns of interaction among the participating groups. The occasions and mechanisms most likely to prove sources of policy are the regular and recurring administrative devices for committing future production objectives, allotting basic resources, and assigning authority to produce.[8] Participation in policy-making involves engaging in activities that are motivated by the desire to have some effect on policy. It is power, in the final analysis, that dictates whether or not such activities have some effect on the resolution of the policy question to which they are addressed. With a variety of actors contending for influence in the policy process, it seems useful to conceive of a "power arrangement" embracing the structure and dynamics of influence within the policy field, resulting in the making of decisions.[9] In this section the explorations of power in the local community will be continued, with an emphasis on the specific areas in which influence is manifested.

In the second part of the interview schedule, which was discussed earlier in connection with power in the Syracuse community, the respondents were asked to rank the influence of local, state, and federal government officials on the making of decisions relevant to the five local institutions being examined here. The hypothesis is that local units of government exercise autonomous power over fewer aspects of the structure and functioning of local law enforcement, public education, social service, and water pollution abatement agencies than do state and federal units of government. The respondents were asked to evaluate and to rank in order of significance the influence of local, state, and federal government on five areas of organizational activity: funding, establishing training programs and/or standards for professional personnel, defining the scope of the organization, evaluating its operational success, and formulating legal and adminis-trative regulations. To give depth to the analysis, questions were asked about the respondents' communication patterns with general government local officials and with state and federal officials. Also asked was who most frequently initiates this communication. This information gives substantive depth to the conclusions about influence relations presented earlier.

According to Karl Deutsch,

> It is communication, that is, the ability to transmit mes-
> sages and to react to them, that makes organizations; and
> it seems that this is true of organizations of living cells
> in the human body as well as of organizations of pieces of
> machinery in an electronic calculator, as well as of organ-
> izations of thinking human beings in social groups.[10]

The communication process is integrally related to the exertion of influence. As explained in Chapter 1, Deutsch explores the connection between the will, character, and power of a system, person, or organ-ization. He defines character as the more or less stable inner pro-gram of a system, person, or organization, and power as the extent to which it can act out its character. Character, then, is defined as the structure of habits and memories acquired in the past, and power is the ability to impose extrapolations or projections of this inner structure on the environment. The vehicle of imposition is communica-tion or the transmission of information. Deutsch sums up his analysis of these concepts as follows:

> To have power means not to have to give in, and to force
> the environment or the other person to do so. Power in
> this narrow sense is the priority of output over intake,
> the ability to talk instead of listen. In a sense, it is the
> ability to afford not to learn.[11]

As a preliminary step to exploring the relative influence of the three levels of government on the activities of local government units, the respondents working within one of the four units were asked to summarize their communication with each of the following: others working within the local agency or institution, general government locals, state officials, and federal officials. The average percents for each group of respondents are summarized in Table 18.

As expected, by far the largest share of a decision-maker's communication is with others working within the same organization. More informative in terms of this study are the relative percentages of time spent with general government locals, state officials, and federal officials. The percentages of communication outside the agency devoted to general government locals, state officials, and federal officials, were computed, as shown in Table 19.

Educators divide their extra-agency communication pretty evenly between general government locals and state officials, with a relatively small proportion going to federal officials. Social service officials communicate twice as much with state officials as with locals. Of the four groups studied, social service officials have least communication with federal officials. Law enforcement decision-makers spend half their time with locals and a third with state officials. Of

TABLE 18

Local Government Communication

| Respondents in | Agency | Percent Communicating with | | |
| | | General Government Locals | State Officials | Federal Officials |
|---|---|---|---|---|
| Education | 81 | 9 | 8 | 2 |
| Social service | 66 | 11 | 22 | 1 |
| Law enforcement | 68 | 17 | 11 | 4 |
| Water pollution control | 50 | 30 | 10 | 10 |

TABLE 19

Communication Outside the Agency

| Respondents in | Percent Communicating with | | |
| | General Government Locals | State Officials | Federal Officials |
|---|---|---|---|
| Education | 47 | 41 | 12 |
| Social service | 31 | 64 | 8 |
| Law enforcement | 54 | 33 | 13 |
| Water Pollution control | 60 | 20 | 20 |

the four groups water pollution control officials spend the most time
with local and federal officials and the least with state officials.
The significance of this communication for the purposes here is in
terms of the decisions themselves.

As will be apparent below, these functions vary in the amounts
of interaction between local and state and federal decision-makers
because of differing conceptions of the nature of state and federal
responsibility to them. Law enforcement officials devote the largest
share of their communication to locals. Also, as will be made evident
below, they believe themselves to be more independent of state and
federal influence than do any of the other groups investigated. Educators spend the next greatest share of time with locals. Again, educators
consider themselves far more independent of state and especially of
federal decision-makers than do social service or water pollution
abatement officials. The latter, devoting the greatest share of their
communication to higher level officials, view their functions as particularly state-oriented. They do not believe that their functions are
primarily the responsibility of the locality.

## INITIATION AND DESTINATION OF
## COMMUNICATION FLOW

Before looking at the decisions, the data on the initiation and
destination of communication flow shall be presented. The question
of who initiates communication is, again, an operationalization of
the symmetry or asymmetry of influence relations between actors
in a political system. As Brams suggests, two actors can be considered to be in a power relationship when they appear to be responsive to each other's behavior. When one actor responds more frequently than the other, it can be assumed that the actor responding
less frequently exercises asymmetrical influence over the actor
responding more frequently; when the actors respond with equal frequency, it can be assumed that they are involved in a symmetrical
influence relationship.[12]

The data here shows the frequency with which the respondents
initiate contact as compared to that with which they receive messages
from general government, local, state, and federal officials. Table
20 indicates the symmetry and asymmetry of influence relations based
on the initiation and destination of communication flow. As shown, in
16 cases relations are symmetrical in that the same level of government (6 local, 10 state) is the primary initiator and the primary
destination of mandates. Seven of the cases reflect asymmetrical
relations. Six indicate that the state is the primary initiator, the
local government the primary destination. From this information one

TABLE 20

Initiation and Destination of Communication Flow

| Primary Destination | Primary Initiator | | |
|---|---|---|---|
| | Local | State | Federal |
| Local | 6 | 6 | 1 |
| State | 0 | 10 | 0 |
| Federal | 0 | 0 | 0 |

can conclude that message flow of policy content is primarily state oriented but does not indicate lesser influence on the part of locals.

Table 21 is a four-area breakdown of the initiation/destination tally. In education there are four symmetrical local/local cases and two symmetrical state/state cases. Only one of the seven is asymmetrical, directed from state to local government. Social service also reflects symmetrical relations, though primarily state oriented. Law enforcement is evenly divided between symmetrical local/local relations, symmetrical state/state relations, and asymmetrical state/local relations. The two water pollution control cases are asymmetrical state/local.

## DECISION-MAKING

Five areas of decision-making within an organization were isolated. (See Table 22.) They are, as noted above, funding, establishing training programs and/or standards for professional personnel, defining the scope of the organization, evaluating its operational success, and formulating legal and administrative regulations. The respondents were asked to rank the three levels of government in order of their significance in the making of decisions in these areas. The chi-square tests on all five areas indicate that the data are significant to the 0.01 level. The lambda coefficients range from 0.4 to 0.6, indicating that error reduction ranges from 40 to 60 percent.

### Education

With the exception of regulation locals see themselves as primary, the state as secondary, and the federal government as tertiary in the making of decisions relevant to local education. This

TABLE 21

Four-Area Breakdown of Initiation/
Destination Tally

| Primary Target | Primary Initiator | | |
| --- | --- | --- | --- |
| | Local | State | Federal |
| EDUCATION | | | |
| Local | 4 | 1 | 0 |
| State | 0 | 2 | 0 |
| Federal | 0 | 0 | 0 |
| SOCIAL SERVICE | | | |
| Local | 0 | 1 | 0 |
| State | 0 | 6 | 0 |
| Federal | 0 | 0 | 0 |
| LAW ENFORCEMENT | | | |
| Local | 2 | 2 | 1 |
| State | 0 | 2 | 0 |
| Federal | 0 | 0 | 0 |
| WATER POLLUTION CONTROL | | | |
| Local | 0 | 2 | 0 |
| State | 0 | 0 | 0 |
| Federal | 0 | 0 | 0 |

finding does not perfectly corroborate the communication data (which
indicates that educators find themselves to share equally in their
communication with general government locals and with state officials),
but it does coincide when the communication information is taken in conjunction with the initiation/destination index. This index suggests
that local educators initiate communication with as frequently as they
receive communication from general government locals, state officials,
and federal officials. Also, they send communication to and receive
it from general government locals and state officials with equal frequency. Table 23 presents a summary of the three measures.

# TABLE 22

## Five Areas of Decision-Making Within an Organization

| Ranking | Level of Government | | |
| --- | --- | --- | --- |
| | Local | State | Federal |

### FUNDING

| Ranking | Local | State | Federal |
| --- | --- | --- | --- |
| 1 | 10 | 7 | 1 |
| 2 | 6 | 10 | 2 |
| 3 | 2 | 0 | 14 |

$x^2 = 34.19$; d.f. $= 4$; $p < 0.01$; $\lambda = 0.47$.

### STAFF

| Ranking | Local | State | Federal |
| --- | --- | --- | --- |
| 1 | 10 | 8 | 0 |
| 2 | 5 | 9 | 1 |
| 3 | 1 | 0 | 7 |

$x^2 = 31.16$; d.f. $= 4$; $p < 0.01$; $\lambda = 0.38$.

### SCOPE

| Ranking | Local | State | Federal |
| --- | --- | --- | --- |
| 1 | 5 | 2 | 0 |
| 2 | 2 | 5 | 0 |
| 3 | 0 | 0 | 4 |

$x^2 = 21.34$; d.f. $= 4$; $p < 0.01$; $\lambda = 0.64$.

### EVALUATION

| Ranking | Local | State | Federal |
| --- | --- | --- | --- |
| 1 | 11 | 5 | 0 |
| 2 | 4 | 11 | 1 |
| 3 | 1 | 0 | 12 |

$x^2 = 43.52$; d.f. $= 4$; $p < 0.01$; $\lambda = 0.62$.

### REGULATION

| Ranking | Local | State | Federal |
| --- | --- | --- | --- |
| 1 | 5 | 12 | 1 |
| 2 | 11 | 6 | 1 |
| 3 | 1 | 0 | 11 |

$x^2 = 39.44$; d.f. $= 4$; $p < 0.01$; $\lambda = 0.53$.

TABLE 23

Education Summary

| Entry | General Government Locals | State Officials | Federal Officials |
|---|---|---|---|
| Communication between educators and | 47% | 41% | 12% |
| Initiation/destination index of influence relation between educators and | symmetrical | symmetrical | none |
| Ranking of influence by educators and general government locals on five aspects of decision-making | 1 | 2 | 3 |

## Social Service

Social service officials see themselves as only slightly more significant than state officials. Federal officials are definitely perceived as tertiary in the making of decisions relevant to the operation of the social service agency. Table 24 presents the raw data on which these findings are based. The conclusion (see Table 25) is that social service officials perceive themselves as sharing decision-making with local and state officials. While their communication is state oriented, this fact does not reflect state dominance over locals.

## Law Enforcement

In the five areas of law enforcement decision-making the local government is again primary (see Table 26). Combining this information with the communication and initiation/destination information results in the summary found in Table 27.

## Water Pollution Control

Dominance of the local government is not indicated in water pollution control as it is in the other three areas (see Table 28). The

# TABLE 24

## Social Service Decisions

| Ranking | Level of Government | | |
|---|---|---|---|
| | Local | State | Federal |

### FUNDING

| Ranking | Local | State | Federal |
|---|---|---|---|
| 1 | 7 | 4 | 3 |
| 2 | 2 | 10 | 2 |
| 3 | 4 | 0 | 9 |

$x^2 = 20.05$; d.f. = 4; $p < 0.01$; $\lambda = 0.44$.

### STAFF

| Ranking | Local | State | Federal |
|---|---|---|---|
| 1 | 8 | 6 | 0 |
| 2 | 4 | 8 | 1 |
| 3 | 1 | 0 | 6 |

$x^2 = 25.1$; d.f. = 4; $p < 0.01$; $\lambda = 0.4$.

### SCOPE

| Ranking | Local | State | Federal |
|---|---|---|---|
| 1 | 2 | 4 | 1 |
| 2 | 2 | 3 | 2 |
| 3 | 3 | 0 | 0 |

$x^2 = 5.782$; d.f. = 4; $p > 0.05$; $\lambda = 0.3$.

### EVALUATION

| Ranking | Local | State | Federal |
|---|---|---|---|
| 1 | 7 | 7 | 0 |
| 2 | 3 | 6 | 4 |
| 3 | 3 | 0 | 4 |

$x^2 = 11.67$; d.f. = 4; $p < 0.05$; $\lambda = 0.2$.

### REGULATION

| Ranking | Local | State | Federal |
|---|---|---|---|
| 1 | 2 | 10 | 2 |
| 2 | 5 | 3 | 2 |
| 3 | 3 | 0 | 4 |

$x^2 = 12.31$; d.f. = 4; $< 0.05$; $\lambda = 0.33$.

TABLE 25

Social Service Summary

| Entry | General Govern-ment Locals | State Officials | Federal Officials |
|---|---|---|---|
| Communication between social service officials and | 31% | 64% | 5% |
| Initiation/destination index of influence relations between social service officials and | none | symmetrical | none |
| Ranking of influence by social service officials and general government locals on five aspects of deci-sion-making | 1 | 1 | 2 |

local government is not, however, excluded from the policy process. The summary (Table 29) gives strength to the conclusion of the primacy of the state government. Although the largest share of the respondents' communication is with general government locals, the primary source of communication of policy content is the state.


Conclusion

This study does not include an in-depth analysis of the influence of nongovernment community groups and individuals on the making of decisions relevant to the four policy areas. Context was added to the study, however, by asking whether government (local, state, and federal) or nongovernment community groups or individuals are perceived to be more significant. The findings indicate that the local government officials interviewed perceive themselves to be more significant than local others.

Officials in the four areas divide the major portion of their communication between general government locals and state officials.

# TABLE 26

## Law Enforcement Decisions

| Ranking | Level of Government | | |
|---|---|---|---|
| | Local | State | Federal |

### FUNDING

| Ranking | Local | State | Federal |
|---|---|---|---|
| 1 | 15 | 1 | 0 |
| 2 | 1 | 12 | 0 |
| 3 | 0 | 0 | 13 |

$x^2 = 73.1$; d.f. $= 4$; $p < 0.01$; $\lambda = 0.92$.

### STAFF

| Ranking | Local | State | Federal |
|---|---|---|---|
| 1 | 12 | 4 | 0 |
| 2 | 4 | 9 | 0 |
| 3 | 0 | 0 | 7 |

$x^2 = 43.04$; d.f. $= 4$; $p < 0.01$; $\lambda = 0.6$.

### SCOPE

| Ranking | Local | State | Federal |
|---|---|---|---|
| 1 | 6 | 0 | 1 |
| 2 | 0 | 6 | 0 |
| 3 | 1 | 0 | 4 |

$x^2 = 25.8$; d.f. $= 4$; $p < 0.01$; $\lambda = 0.82$.

### EVALUATION

| Ranking | Local | State | Federal |
|---|---|---|---|
| 1 | 12 | 3 | 0 |
| 2 | 3 | 6 | 1 |
| 3 | 0 | 1 | 8 |

$x^2 = 31.7$; d.f. $= 4$; $p < 0.01$; $\lambda = 0.58$.

### REGULATION

| Ranking | Local | State | Federal |
|---|---|---|---|
| 1 | 8 | 6 | 2 |
| 2 | 5 | 8 | 1 |
| 3 | 3 | 0 | 9 |

$x^2 = 20.37$; d.f. $= 4$; $p < 0.01$; $\lambda = 0.35$.

TABLE 27

Law Enforcement Summary

| Entry | General Govern- ment Locals | State Officials | Federal Officials |
|---|---|---|---|
| Communication between law enforcement officials and | 54% | 33% | 13% |
| Initiation/desti- nation index of influence rela- tions between law enforcement offi- cials and | symmetrical | asymmetrical | asymmetrical |
| Ranking of influence by law enforce- ment officials and general government locals on five aspects of decision-making | 1 | 1 | 2 |

The smallest share of their total communication, ranging from 5 percent for the social service officials to 20 percent for those involved
in water pollution control, is with federal officials. The symmetry/
asymmetry calculation of policy-oriented message flow suggests
that, while the state government is most frequently the originator of
such messages, it is also most frequently the recipient of like messages
originating with local officials. Thus, it was concluded that relations
between local and state officials are symmetrical. General government locals are bypassed to some extent, but this does not mean that
power is out of the hands of all locals. It is the functionary (i.e., the
superintendent of schools, the chief of police, or the commissioner
of social service), rather than the mayor, the county executive, or
the local legislator, who shares influence with the state official, but
it is still the local official. One can say, then, that the communication
flow between influentials of local government units and influentials
of extracommunity government units involved in the same social function is symmetrical.

TABLE 28

Water Pollution Control Decisions

| Ranking | Level of Government | | |
|---------|-------|-------|---------|
|         | State | Local | Federal |
| FUNDING | | | |
| 1 | 3 | 5 | 2 |
| 2 | 3 | 5 | 2 |
| 3 | 4 | 0 | 5 |
| STAFF | | | |
| 1 | 3 | 1 | 0 |
| 2 | 1 | 2 | 0 |
| 3 | 0 | 0 | 0 |
| SCOPE | | | |
| 1 | 2 | 0 | 0 |
| 2 | 0 | 2 | 0 |
| 3 | 0 | 0 | 2 |
| EVALUATION | | | |
| 1 | 3 | 3 | 0 |
| 2 | 2 | 3 | 1 |
| 3 | 1 | 0 | 3 |
| REGULATION | | | |
| 1 | 1 | 7 | 2 |
| 2 | 2 | 3 | 5 |
| 3 | 7 | 0 | 1 |

Using Deutsch's terminology, decisions were defined in five areas of organizational relevance as currencies of political interchange. These decisions concern funding, staffing, defining the scope of, evaluating, and regulating the local agency. With the exception of water pollution control, it was concluded that currency flow is symmetrical. Locals and state officials have an equal share of the responsibility for decision-making.

TABLE 29

Water Pollution Control Summary

| Entry | General Govern- ment Locals | State Officials | Federal Officials |
|---|---|---|---|
| Communication between water pollution con- trol officials and | 60% | 20% | 20% |
| Initiation/destination index of influence relations between water pollution officials and | none | asymmetrical (state) | none |
| Ranking of influence by water pollution control officials and general government locals on five aspects of decision- making | 2 | 1 | 3 |

Two major hypotheses for the study as a whole are as follows: (a) local units of government exercise autonomous power over fewer aspects of the structure and function of local law enforcement, public education, social service, and water pollution control agencies than do state and federal units of government; and (b) the greatest share of decision-making within these areas relevant to the community is made by government officials at the state and federal levels. The authors have not been able to confirm these hypotheses. The evidence suggests that, with the exception of the water pollution control agency, local units of government share power and decision-making equally with the state government. The federal government, of course, mani- fests itself through the state government to a great extent. To the extent that federal officials interact directly with locals, their influence on policy is decidedly tertiary. As stated above, an exploration of the state-federal relation in these functional areas is considered to be beyond the scope of this study.

# 7

## THE PARTICIPANTS
## IN THE POLICY PROCESS

There is little doubt that innumerable groups and players contend for influence in the governmental policy-making arena. They include parties, public officials, the bureaucracy, special interest groups, and various publics. Political leaders and private influentials have received considerable attention in discussions of community power, but the governmental bureaucracy has usually been overlooked. This is a serious failing in the community power literature, for bureaucracy is being pushed toward a position of preeminence in the governmental process. By virtue of numbers alone the bureaucracy constitutes a force in government that cannot be ignored. In 1967 local government accounted for somewhat more than half of all civilian public employment, with over 5.5 million full-time equivalent employees.[1] The pressures generated by increasing urbanization for new and expanded public services have swelled the ranks of local government; and the large, industrial, and complex nature of society has enhanced the reputation of the professional civil servant.

The bureaucracy has become more important because of a growing need for expertise in government at the metropolitan level. The general tendency in business and government is for the bureaucracy to become more influential as issues and problems become increasingly complex and as large organizations depend more and more on organizational decision-making processes.[2] As functional activities become more dependent on science and technology, political officials are compelled to rely increasingly on the knowledge, specialized skills, and advice of professional personnel.

This characteristic of bureaucratic organization was early noted by scholars:

> The decisive reason for the advance of bureaucratic
> organization has always been its purely technical
> superiority over any other form of organization. . . .

Under nominal conditions, the power position of a fully developed bureaucracy is always overpowering. The 'political master' finds himself in a position of the 'dilettante' who stands opposite the 'expert,' facing the trained official who stands within the management of administration.[3]

A decisive power of initiative has been moving into the hands of executive officials, who, as amateurs in the many technological aspects of community functioning, find it more and more difficult to challenge policy advice based on specialized knowledge. The continuity and sustained attention of the civil servant allows him a considerable advantage in framing policy decisions over political officials who deal with a wide variety of problems and confront each issue of public policy only at sporadic intervals.[4] This advantage has been offset somewhat at the national level with the committee system and seniority provisions among legislative policy-makers, but nothing comparable has developed at the local level. In fact, most urban legislative officials (city councilmen) hold only part-time positions, further aggravating their disadvantage.

It is the professional who is at the growing edge of policy and who provides most of the energy and innovation in the policy process. Professionals are primarily committed to the attainment of the goals that their skills are designed to achieve, and their specialization gives them not only problem-solving capabilities but also foresight. Professionalism both raises the standards of performance of activities and rigidifies the hierarchy of administration, resulting in islands of power largely beyond the control of outside forces.[5] In certain areas—science and national defense at the federal level and health and hospitals at the state and local level—the expertise and informational resources of bureaucracy have themselves been the controlling factors in the development of public policy. As one author puts it, "The development of public policy and the methods of administration owed less in the long run to processes of conflict among political parties and social and economic pressure groups than to the more objective processes of research and discussion among professional groups."[6]

Bureaucratic influence, however, is by no means a constant factor in the policy process. A variety of factors, including the policy area involved, the degree of technology required, and the existence of organized and skilled opposition, determines the degree of bureaucratic power. The bureaucratic structure of government in urban areas is not monolithic, encompassing all public personnel within its administrative fold. It is instead highly pluralistic, like other interested groups and like government itself, each agency or unit having its own entrenched officials, employees, and jurisdictions.[7]

Although bureaucratic forces contend with numerous groups in the urban arena for resources and support, one of their key characteristics is the search for autonomy. Encouraged perhaps by the early reform drives to remove politics and corruption from administration, civil servants have been able to isolate themselves from policy-makers at the center of government. This situation hides the fact, however, that independent decision-makers still make decisions that are political, that is, that involve policy. Nevertheless, both bureaucracies and their clientele naturally believe theirs to be a special aspect of government to which others may not be equally sympathetic, and they strive to insulate themselves from larger political forces.[8] The success of such efforts is indicated to a degree by elected officials who find it necessary to reassure the public that they are not interfering improperly when they attempt to decide some aspects of policy.

The ability to cultivate political support is another aspect of bureaucratic influence. Agencies have power when they command the allegiance of fervent and substantial constituencies and when they provide channels of access through which segments of the public can advance or protect their interests.[9] As Norton Long says, "The bureaucracy under the American political system has a large share of responsibility for the public promotion of policy and even more in organizing the political basis for its survival and growth."[10] Thus, bureaucrats are in a commanding position over the shape of public policy not only because they possess the necessary professional skills but also because they are able to structure the public attitudes and preferences to which their policy decisions are in theory supposed to respond.[11]

The traditional view of the role of public administrators affords an additional perspective into bureaucratic power. Historically considered separate from the policy-making process, administrators were to execute and implement the policies determined by elected officials. Recent students of public policy, however, have come to understand that its making and execution are inseparably intertwined. While genuine policies, as distinguished from generalized aims, come into being through the activities of an entire organization, it is the people who cooperate in implementing policies who give them meaning and content. Paul Appleby defines the role of the administrator:

> Administration is the application of policy formulated by law in a constantly unfolding process, making the laws of legislators and the courts increasingly more specific by means of policy formulations and determinations applied to particular publics, to smaller publics, and finally to individual cases.[12]

Bureaucracies may not have monopoly power over policy-making, but obviously they play a strategic role in the process by which decisions are made. The bureaucracies now have the status and the capacity of autonomous participants in the city's political process.13 Their professional capabilities give them a key position in policy innovation, and their discretionary authority in interpreting and executing provides wide latitude for maneuver and redefinition. A great deal of the work of civil servants consists of preparing policy proposals and implementing them once they have been formally endorsed. No one can rule without the bureaucracy, if for no other reason than its enormous capacity for "nondecision," the ability to keep certain matters from coming to decision at all.14

As government jurisdictions become more urbanized, the need for bureaucratic expertise grows, and bureaucratic politics rather than party politics becomes the dominant theater of decision. The four policy areas chosen for examination in this report reveal this trend. The policy process in one area, water pollution control, has been extensively examined and will provide the major source of data for this section. Each of the other three areas—law enforcement, social service, and education—will, however, be the subject of an introductory discussion in the following pages.

## LAW ENFORCEMENT POLICY-MAKING

The traditional view of law enforcement policy is quite straight-forward. Laws are adopted by legislators or fashioned by the courts and enforced by the police and the courts. In theory, the police are supposed to have almost no discretion; they are required to enforce all laws equally everywhere. In fact, as has come to be recognized, police discretion is inevitable because of the impossibility of observing all infractions of the law and the necessity of interpreting or applying the law in a specific situation. Also, in the final analysis, the police believe that public opinion would not tolerate full enforcement of all laws all the time.15 If such discretion in decision-making exists for the police patrolman, if community choices rarely affect police behavior in arrest and detention, what about the larger policy questions involving resources, organizational change, and priorities? How and by whom are such decisions affecting police policy made?

The actors involved in the law enforcement policy process include the mayor or city manager, city council members, the police chief, policemen (usually through their police benevolent associations), lawyers, and citizen groups. Formally, decisions as to resources and priorities are made by the chief executive and the legislature. As indicated by most research and consistent with the earlier discussion, however, most policy questions are decided by police chiefs. Thus, the decision-making theater is located among organizational forces. John A. Gardiner suggests that police chiefs alone decide, within very broad limits, what traffic law enforcement policy a city will have.16 Neither political intervention nor particular community characteristics seem to have any large influence over this policy question.

Although the police role is not yet recognized as a professional one, the police have gained a large degree of autonomy. The demand to remove corruption and politics from law enforcement has provided a wide scope for police officials in establishing police policy. The police have been able to insulate themselves from community decision-making influences, predominantly through the cultivation of political support for independence. Although most police activity does not involve a high degree of technology, the police official has an advantage over political policy-makers in his experience and mastery of law. And the development of patrolmen's associations has further contributed to organizational determinism by establishing certain limits within which policemen will cooperate in law enforcement. One author suggests that the mayor of New York has to fight a running battle to maintain some control over the police department: "The political power of the department is such that all mayors have to keep reassuring the public they are not interfering improperly when they attempt to decide police policy."17

The authors do not mean to suggest that community choice is absent from police decision-making. Police are sensitive to and concerned about the public. But the absence of general citizen interest and the particularistic nature of political interest limit the direct influence of citizen policy-makers. As one author indicates,

> to be governed is to submit to deliberate and systematic
> determination, by someone in authority, matters of
> policy, operating procedure and organizational objectives.
> The policies described in this study—handling petty offenses
> and traffic violations, treating juveniles—are, with very
> few exceptions, determined by the police themselves with-
> out any deliberate or systematic intervention by political
> authorities."18

### SOCIAL SERVICE POLICY-MAKING

In recent years state and federal governments have taken over from local governments the direction and financing of public assistance programs. The Great Depression brought about federal intervention

on a broad scale and turned the predominantly private and local
welfare efforts into an intergovernmental welfare program.  For 30
years local governments have been administering public assistance
programs while sharing the financing and policy-making with state
and federal governments.  One author has characterized this process
as automated, with legislative bodies providing little input or program
evaluation beyond the yearly appropriation of funds.[19]  He goes on to
point out that strong interest-group participation does not characterize
public assistance policy-making.  Unlike client groups of law enforcement and education, the recipients of welfare are powerless.  Gilbert
Steiner says, "Those who can be heard do not have a great deal to
gain or lose.  Those with a great deal to gain or lose cannot be heard,"
and, "There is no ready sanction available to the client.  He has
nothing to withhold."[20]  On the other hand, professional groups that
might provide leadership, such as the American Public Welfare
Association and the National Association of Social Workers, have
failed to influence the policy-making process.  Thus, from a political
perspective the policy process in the social services is, to a considerable extent, automated in both legislative and administrative areas,
dominated by the past and lacking vigorous competing influences.

At the local level the locus of power over public assistance
policy has shifted.  With increased federal and state financing the
discretion of local officials, executive and legislative, has decreased,
and the role of civil servants and administrators in the social services
has become dominant.  As Harold Wilensky and Charles Lebeaux
observe:

> Those public welfare executives and technicians who are
> program minded, in collaboration with relevant pressure
> groups, clearly affect much welfare policy.  They have the
> technical knowledge and experience which their political
> superiors and legislative committees lack; they can use
> both executive and legislative channels to shape welfare
> programs.  Such experts, grouped in formidable bureau-
> cracies, also bridge the wide gulf between legislative
> "policy" and "execution;" they do not make policy, but
> they crystallize the policy when the policy is loose,
> sharpen the definition of the problem when its specificity
> is low, fill the vacuum when the boss is busy or time ıs
> short, use official policy pronouncements as a lever to
> strengthen and broaden welfare programs.[21]

To the extent that discretion is available locally, it belongs to
professional administrators, mostly to the head of the agency.  It is
his values and preferences that are expressed in the local government's

application of state and federal laws and rules. This shifting locus
of power is evidenced not only in public welfare agencies. As social
work has grown more professional and agencies more specialized,
board members and legislative policy-makers have largely withdrawn
from participation in agency operations and do not exercise their
policy-making powers except to get very broad limits as to direction
and scale of agency effort. The executive of a family service agency
wrote several years ago:

> I've been concerned and at the same time both amused and
> somewhat guilty about the fact that the Board of Directors
> makes policy decisions, both by authority of the by-laws
> and in the actual voting they do; yet actually in the present
> day family casework agency the staff has to "educate" the
> Board constantly and persistently and it certainly does
> choose the elements of education which lead toward the
> conclusions of which the staff approves. In other words,
> we tell them how to vote and they vote, and we call that
> process 'the Board sets the policies of the agency.'[22]

Local welfare directors, like the police chief, are sensitive to
and shaped by community experiences and preferences. But the
automated character of the intergovernmental welfare programs and
the constraints placed upon local governmental units by state and
federal rules limit the direct policy influences of formal community
policy-makers. Local welfare administrators exercise relatively
little discretion in following state and federal norms, but such discretion as they do exercise seems to be in accordance with their
own preferences.[23]

## EDUCATIONAL POLICY-MAKING

As in the case of the police function, citizen demands have
resulted in the establishment of independent governing units for
local education. The reform movement, with its emphasis on apolitical
administrative efficiency and objectivity, has led to local schools
having separate governing boards, elected or appointed, insulated
from central government policy-making except perhaps with regard
to general budgetary levels. Although the formal institutional
description of power and prerogatives may lead one to believe that
the school board plays a decisive role in school policy-making, board
members actually constitute only one force in the complex policy
process, which includes school superintendents, central staffs,
education associations, university groups, and citizen organizations

such as the PTA. Study after study suggests that all these forces
contend with one another for influence in the educational policy
arena.

Nevertheless, the school superintendent and the central staff
appear to dominate most spheres of urban and suburban school policy.
The superintendent exercises influence by defining school issues,
proposing acceptable alternatives, providing ammunition for his
supporters, and, in the end, implementing or not implementing the
decisions.24 As Roscoe Martin puts it, "He [the superintendent] is
as much a policy maker as he is a manager in the narrow sense; for
he enjoys an expertise, a professional reputation, and a community
position which combine to give him almost an irresistible voice in
school affairs."25

Studies of education in the city consistently reveal that educational
policy-making is an isolated process, insulated from significant
influence on the part of other community officers or citizens. An
execeptional issue for which there is wide public support is that of
the independence of educational units, which, it is felt, since they
deal with children, should be kept out of politics. One study reports
that relatively few public school policy proposals entertained by
legislators resulted from general public pressures or intense public
protests. The authors suggested the existence of a "subtle pyramiding
of power in terms of who articulates demands. This power lies
predominantly in the hands of the official spokesmen of the organized
interests, the professionals, who are limited only by what the political
system will allow or by what they think it will allow."26

School officials usually have influence over internal issues,
those that require little negotiation with elements in the political
structure outside the schools. And for the most part it is the
superintendent and central staff, through research and negotiation,
who structure the forces in the policy arena so that specific proposals
relating to external issues are adopted.27 The school board exercises
power of legitimation, but in most instances members are part-time
officials who have no expertise, little staff, and no access to the
performance criteria or data upon which to question the judgment of
the superintendent and his staff. Those issues with a more intense
audience appeal, such as integration, sex education, and the neighborhood
school, are primarily the responsibility of the school board because
the educational professional considers them to be "political" issues.

Teachers' associations, which have key influence potential in
the policy process, have concerned themselves so far with staff
benefits and responsibilities rather than with curricula, facilities,
or programs. And parent-teacher associations, set up in conjunction
with local school systems, generally play a supportive or permissive
role toward school officials, relying mainly on information from the

school bureaucracy for discussion and not having the continuous attention or sufficient expertise to exert a positive influence on school policy.

In sum, educational policy-making is characterized by a predominant influence on the part of school superintendents and/or central staff, a more passive and formal decision-making role played by school boards (except in crucial community issues), a potentially important yet presently specialized role for teachers' associations, and a limited influence for other community officers and citizens, generally in the area of budgetary limits.

## WATER POLLUTION CONTROL POLICY-MAKING

Unlike that of the other three policy areas examined, the history of pollution abatement agencies and programs is relatively brief. The following chapters employ a schema similar to the one used in the discussions above, that is, examining the role of the public, individuals, and institutions in the policy-making process. They present a detailed case study of water pollution policy-making and of the complex interaction among individuals and groups that characterizes the policy process.

## CHAPTER 8

**PUBLIC OPINION
AND THE INFLUENTIALS**

If one is interested in linking community power to community policy, it is necessary to concern oneself with the preferences of the community and its leaders. Thus, it was in exploring the dynamics of policy-making that power relations and community opinion were investigated. As noted in an earlier chapter, public opinion seldom influences public policy directly. At election time the role of the public is decisive in selecting policy-makers, but rarely are representatives given any particular policy mandate. Between elections public opinion plays a relatively passive role, supportive or permissive in setting general limits—"opinion dikes"—to government action but leaving much discretion in policy-making to officials.[1]

It is the interaction between the public and its leaders that is the concern here. Little research has been done on the preferences of opinion leaders, political activists, or influentials. A variety of factors, among them the generality of public preferences, the low intensity of the opinions of many people, and the slow process of translating disapproval of specific policies into electoral reprisal, contributes to the wide latitude for creative leadership among this group and gives credence to the necessity of exploring the interaction between general public preferences and the views and opinions of leaders.[2] But it is inadequate to conceive of the political structure as consisting of political officials only, for the ranks of the activists include a broad spectrum of political participants—the expert, the amateur, the concerned.

## ATTITUDES TOWARD WATER POLLUTION

In seeking to define this complex interaction of communication, in which political influentials both affect mass opinion and are

conditioned by it, the authors extensively explored the opinions of a
sample of a single community concerning one policy area, water
pollution control, and related the findings to the positions of activists
in the same area. The interest was in comparing the cognitions,
priorities, and preferences of this elite with the public at large in the
community. The sample public used for this research is the same as
that used in an earlier section of this report, consisting of 1,036 respondents randomly selected from the Syracuse SMSA.* The sample
of influentials chosen for interviewing provided a heterogeneous group
coming from both the executive and the legislative branches of county
government and from some of the professions and interest groups in
the county, all either directly involved in the policy process or so
close to it that they can evaluate competently certain aspects of the
water pollution control policy process and its relation to community
opinion.**

It was seen in Chapter 5 that water pollution is generally regarded by the residents of Onondaga County as a social problem less
pressing than education and law enforcement but more pressing than
most other local issues. The finding is interesting in that, although
the problem of water pollution in the county is obvious and relatively
well understood, it is still not regarded as the most urgent of public
questions. It is unusual that water pollution is considered a middle-
level priority, while parks and recreational facilities are of the lowest
order of preference in both measurements.

Why should county residents be less concerned with parks and
recreational facilities than they are with water pollution when it seems
that the polluted waters are, or at least would be, used primarily for
recreational purposes? Three reasons might account for this apparent
paradox. First, water pollution is probably interpreted primarily as
a potential threat to the well-being of residents rather than as an
inhibition to recreation. Second, water pollution is obvious and may
offend the aesthetic senses of residents without their being interested
in the lake and its feeding streams for recreational purposes. Water
pollution may have received attention in the local media to the degree
that residents are concerned about it without necessarily connecting
it with aesthetics or recreational facilities. Finally, it may simply
be that large numbers of local residents are against water pollution
because it seems a simple, understandable, and noncontroversial
thing to be against. To attempt to answer some of these questions

---

*See Chapter 5 for sample data.

**See Figure for a list of individuals interviewed.

and to measure attitudes toward water pollution in a more precise way, some additional questions were asked.

## Onondaga Lake as a Recreational Resource

Interest in Onondaga Lake as a recreational resource was measured by two questions. The first, as Table 30 indicates, concerned using the lake for swimming and boating, while the second concerned the lake as supporting fish and other animal life such as water fowl. In both instances the sample responded strongly for action on the part of county governments to improve the lake. Slightly more than 85 percent of the residents either agree or strongly agree that county governments should clean the lake for swimming and boating; 88 percent agree or strongly agree about supporting fish and animal life. It appears that the lake is regarded as a recreation source, although this generalization should be made cautiously because the questions were worded in a way that suggested this use. A much safer generalization from the responses to these questions is that county residents strongly feel that government should make the lake clean and safe for recreation.

## The Citizen's Involvement

Not only do residents connect the lake with recreation and feel that the governments of the county should make it usable for recreation purposes but they also feel that water pollution affects them directly. When asked to respond to, "Pollution is a problem which doesn't affect me at all," 80 percent either disagreed or strongly disagreed. Thus, without being precise about how they are affected by water pollution these people indicate that they do feel affected.

## The Financial Aspect

Two statements were posed on financing the elimination of water pollution in the Onondaga watershed, one of which was, "Ending pollution of Onondaga Lake would be too expensive to be worthwhile." As Table 30 indicates, 59 percent of the respondents disagreed or strongly disagreed. Almost one-third (31 percent), however, were unable to make a judgment as to whether the costs of ending pollution would be commensurate with the benefits.

Each person in the sample was asked to indicate the amount of money he would be willing to pay in extra taxes each year for the

## TABLE 30

### Attitudes Toward Water Pollution
### (in percent)

| Response | Question* | | | |
| --- | --- | --- | --- | --- |
| | 1 | 2 | 3 | 4 |
| Strongly agree | 44 | 43 | 3 | 3 |
| Agree | 43 | 45 | 6 | 18 |
| Don't know | 6 | 5 | 31 | 7 |
| Disagree | 5 | 2 | 41 | 52 |
| Strongly disagree | 1 | 1 | 18 | 28 |

*The questions are:

1. "If Onondaga Lake is unhealthful for swimming and boating, the County should do whatever is necessary to make it safe for recreation."

2. "If Onondaga Lake is not clean enough for fish and animals to live in, the County should clean it up."

3. "Ending pollution of Onondaga Lake would be too expensive to be worthwhile."

4. "Pollution is a problem which doesn't affect me at all."

next ten years to end totally water pollution in the county. In reply, 22 percent stated they would be willing to spend $3, 16 percent would give $5, 25 percent would spend $10, 6 percent would pay $15, and 14 percent would pay $20. From the responses to these questions there appears to be, first, a general feeling that it would not be too costly to end water pollution; second, a willingness to spend for such activities; and third, wide variation in the amount each resident is prepared to pay to stop pollution.

Altogether, the responses to these questions seem to indicate the following general attitudes toward water pollution in Onondaga County: People feel it to be a middle-level public problem that affects them directly; they feel that governments in the county should do what is necessary to solve this problem; and they are willing to pay for it, although in varying amounts.

## CORRELATES OF ATTITUDES TOWARD
## WATER POLLUTION

Several additional factors were considered for each respondent in an attempt to account for some of the variation in attitudes toward

water pollution and its control. Notations were made as to the sex
and place of residence of the respondent. In addition, each respondent
was asked his age (in some instances estimates were made), the
education level of the head of the household, and the approximate annual
family income (in categories of $3,000 to $7,000, $7,000 to $10,000,
$10,000 to $15,000, and $15,000 and above). These data were an
attempt to answer such questions as the following: How does education
influence attitudes toward water pollution? What power does income
have over the willingness to spend for pollution control? Does living
inside the central city give a different perspective of the problem?
Is age a salient determinant of views on pollution?

### The Urban-Suburban Differential

Do persons living inside the central city have a different view
than their suburban counterparts of the priority of water pollution
control vis-à-vis the other social problems with which government
deals? When using the free selection technique, differences do
appear, as Table 31 shows. On the basis of simple ranking of importance associated with these problems, city and suburban respondents
agreed that education is the most pressing, followed by police protection. For the third-order priority, however, city respondents selected
employment, while suburbanites chose water pollution. It is not surprising that city residents place employment (third) and housing
(fourth) before water pollution control (fifth), because the central
cities are the loci of the majority of deteriorated housing and ghetto
conditions, as well as the homes of those who are most likely to regard work and its availability as a pressing question. It seems most
unusual, however, that city residents relegate welfare to seventh
place in the group of ten, while suburban respondents rank it sixth!
Suburbanites, by contrast, place housing low (eighth), whereas those
in the central city place it fourth.

On the basis of statistical significance city and suburban respondents differ on housing, water pollution, maintenance of streets,
welfare, water adequacy, and park and recreational facilities. City
residents attach greater importance to housing, street maintenance,
welfare, and park and recreational facilities than do suburbanites.
Conversely, suburban respondents regard water pollution and adequacy
as more important. Some probable sources of this difference can be
suggested. More suburban residents are secure in their housing and
employment than are their urban equivalents. In this state of need
satisfaction suburbanites rank pure water for drinking, aesthetics,
and recreation as more important, whereas more city residents are
still seeking housing and employment goals. Once housing and

TABLE 31

Relative Importance Associated with Alternative
Areas of Public Policy, by Urban
and Suburban Residence

| City Priority Ranking | Suburban Priority Ranking |
|---|---|
| Education | Education |
| Police protection | Police protection |
| Employment | Water pollution |
| Housing | Employment |
| Water pollution | Adequate water |
| Maintenance of streets | Welfare |
| Welfare | Maintenance of streets |
| Adequate water | Housing |
| Parks and recreational facilities | Traffic tie-ups |
| Traffic tie-ups | Parks and recreational facilities |

| Policy Area | Most Important | Somewhat Less Important | Least Important |
|---|---|---|---|
| Education | | | |
| City (N=478) | 80 | 13 | 7 |
| Suburb (N=558) | 83 | 13 | 4 |
| Police protection | | | |
| City | 70 | 16 | 14 |
| Suburb | 71 | 20 | 9 |
| Employment | | | |
| City | 57 | 31 | 12 |
| Suburb | 51 | 32 | 17 |
| Housing | | | |
| City | 54$^b$ | 33 | 13 |
| Suburb | 27 | 41 | 32 |
| Water pollution | | | |
| City | 50$^b$ | 38 | 12 |
| Suburb | 63 | 23 | 14 |
| Maintenance of streets | | | |
| City | 48$^b$ | 36 | 16 |
| Suburb | 34 | 44 | 22 |
| Welfare | | | |
| City | 45$^a$ | 34 | 21 |
| Suburb | 37 | 34 | 28 |
| Adequate water | | | |
| City | 34$^b$ | 29 | 27 |
| Suburb | 51 | 24 | 24 |
| Parks and rec. facil. | | | |
| City | 28$^b$ | 48 | 24 |
| Suburb | 24 | 39 | 33 |
| Traffic tie-ups | | | |
| City | 29 | 33 | 38 |
| Suburb | 26 | 33 | 41 |

[a]Statistically significant at the 0.01 level of confidence.
[b]Statistically significant at the 0.001 level of confidence.

employment requirements are satisfied, people are more free to focus
on the need for water for recreation and beauty.

### Age, Education, and Income Differentials

The influence of age, education, and income on the free selection
of water pollution priorities gives further insights. As Table 32 shows,
there is no statistically significant difference between those above and
below 40 years of age and between those with a high school education
or less and those with some college. Income, however, does influence
the salience attached to water pollution as a problem, those with higher
incomes regarding it as more important than do those with lower
incomes. It appears, then, that locational and economic factors are
more likely to influence the public on water policy issues than are
age and educational factors. It also appears that public policies that
call for pollution abatement are likely to receive greater support
among those who are better off and live in the suburbs.

As described earlier, the general response to the statement,
"If Onondaga Lake is unhealthful for swimming and boating, the county
should do whatever is necessary to make it safe for recreation," was
agreement or strong agreement. When broken down by age, place of
residence, education, and income, the responses differ only slightly,
as Table 33 shows. Younger persons, those with some college, and
members of families with annual incomes of more than $7,000 indicate
moderately stronger feelings than older persons, less educated persons,
and those from lower income families on the necessity for the county
to make the lake safe for recreation. These variances are not
statistically significant, however, leading to the conclusion that there
is such a general level of agreement upon this question that moderate
variations on the basis of age, education, or income are not particularly
meaningful.

### The Contributors to Pollution

As described above, both industry and government contribute
to the pollution of water in the Onondaga drainage basin. Because
both are so involved, it would be difficult either to argue or to demonstrate that one is more guilty than the other. Nevertheless, it is
interesting to probe the attitudes of the residents of the county on
what they regard as the relative amounts of water pollution resulting
from sewage or industrial waste. The statement was proposed:
"Industries pollute Onondaga Lake much more than does public sewage."
As might be anticipated, a large percentage of the respondents stated

TABLE 32

Influence of Age, Education, and Income
on Importance Associated with Water
Pollution as Public Problem
(in percent)
(N=1036)

| Importance | Age | | Education | | Income | |
|---|---|---|---|---|---|---|
| | 39 or Under N-504 | 40 or Above N-532 | O=12 Years N=626 | Some College N=410 | Under $7,000 N-424 | Above $7,000 N-612 |
| Most important N=586 | 52 | 58 | 53 | 56 | 53 | 60* |
| Somewhat less important N=327 | 34 | 29 | 30 | 31 | 34 | 28 |
| Least important N=123 | 12 | 11 | 13 | 12 | 11 | 11 |

*Statistically significant at the 0.05 level of confidence.

they did not know (42 percent). Still, 42 percent either agree or
strongly agree that industry is more at fault than government, while
only 15 percent disagree or strongly disagree with the statement. It
appears, then, that industry is more often than government considered to be the culprit. It should be noted here, however, that the
wording of the question might have resulted in a "response set" in the
direction of agreeing that industries are more at fault.

When the responses to this question are broken down by age,
residence, education, and income, some variation is found, as Table
33 indicates. For instance, those living in the city and those with
less education are more inclined to take a position on the question
rather than to state that they do not know. Neither age nor residence
noticeably influences attitudes toward the source of pollution, except
for the greater reluctance of suburbanites to take a position on the
question and their tendency to disagree with the statement that industry is more at fault. Those with a high school education or less
are more inclined both to take a stand on the question and to regard
industry as being "more guilty" than are those with some college,
but the difference is not significant. On the other hand, those from
families making more than $7,000 yearly are slightly more inclined
to consider industry as a greater polluter than are those from families
making less, but again there is no significant difference.

TABLE 33

Influence of Age, Residence, Education, and Income on
Agreement with Three Questions on Water Pollution
(N=1036)
(in percent)

| Question | Age | | Residence | | Education | | Income | | Agreement |
|---|---|---|---|---|---|---|---|---|---|
| | Under 40 N=504 | Over 40 N=532 | City N=478 | Suburb N=558 | 0-12 Years N=626 | Some College N=410 | Under $7000 N=424 | Above $7,000 N=612 | |
| If Onondaga Lake is unhealthful for swimming and boating, the County should do whatever is necessary to make it safe for recreation. | 48 | 41 | 36 | 43 | 44 | 48 | 39 | 47 | Strongly agree |
| | 42 | 44 | 43 | 43 | 40 | 41 | 47 | 41 | Agree |
| | 5 | 6 | 6 | 6 | 7 | 5 | 7 | 5 | Don't know |
| | 4 | 5 | 4 | 5 | 5 | 3 | 5 | 5 | Disagree |
| | 0.4 | 2 | 0.8 | 1 | 2 | 0.7 | 0.9 | 1 | Strongly disagree |
| Chemical industries pollute Onondaga Lake much more than does public sewage. | 17 | 20 | 17[a] | 20 | 25 | 16 | 20 | 18 | Strongly agree |
| | 27 | 23 | 25 | 24 | 25 | 24 | 19 | 26 | Agree |
| | 41 | 40 | 37 | 44 | 36 | 44 | 42 | 40 | Don't know |
| | 11 | 11 | 14 | 9 | 11 | 12 | 15 | 12 | Disagree |
| | 3 | 4 | 5 | 2 | 2 | 4 | 3 | 3 | Strongly disagree |
| Pollution of Onondaga Lake is a problem which doesn't affect me at all. | 1 | 4[b] | 2 | 3 | 5 | 2[b] | 5 | 1[b] | Strongly agree |
| | 6 | 15 | 9 | 11 | 16 | 7 | 15 | 6 | Agree |
| | 4 | 10 | 7 | 6 | 12 | 4 | 13 | 4 | Don't know |
| | 59 | 44 | 52 | 51 | 47 | 49 | 48 | 51 | Disagree |
| | 29 | 25 | 28 | 27 | 18 | 36 | 19 | 36 | Strongly disagree |

[a]Statistically significant at the 0.01 level of confidence.
[b]Statistically significant at the 0.001 level of confidence.

120

A great majority of the respondents feel that water pollution in the county is a problem that affects them. As Table 33 shows, there is some variation in this point of view on the basis of differences in age, education, and income. Persons above 40 feel considerably less affected by pollution than do their younger counterparts. (In the free selection priority preferences those above 40 regard water pollution as more important than do those below 40. Here they state they feel less affected by pollution. This is not necessarily a contradiction.) The same is true for those with a high school education or less and for those whose family incomes are lower than $7,000 annually. Thus, although there is a tendency for the respondents to feel affected by water pollution, those who are older, less educated, and less well off do not feel as strongly or directly affected. These findings suggest that older persons may be less interested than younger persons in the water of the county for recreational purposes and therefore may not feel so directly affected by its pollution, although they regard it as an important public priority. Those with less education and income may be more likely to regard water pollution as a less direct concern of theirs because they are not in a financial position to utilize the waters for recreational purposes or to appreciate their aesthetic qualities.

It was stated above that the respondents generally feel that governments in the county should do what is necessary to solve water pollution problems and that they are willing to pay for the solution, although in varying amounts. Table 34 indicates what percentage of respondents are willing to be taxed at particular levels to solve the problem. From an examination of Table 34 the following generalizations are valid. First, a higher level of education is associated with a greater willingness to be taxed at higher amounts to attempt to control water pollution. Second, place of residence produces no clear contrast of the willingness of the city and suburban residents to be taxed to pay for the elimination of pollution. At the center categories, from $3 to $15, city and suburban residents are almost identical in their willingness to be taxed, but at the extremes, $0 and $20, city residents are considerably more willing to be taxed to support pollution control than are their suburban counterparts. Third, those over 40 seem notably less willing to pay for improved water quality than those below 40. Finally, higher levels of income are clearly associated with a greater predisposition to favor increased taxation for water pollution control.

## Conclusion

A basic conclusion to be drawn from the findings of this research is that water pollution is generally regarded as a serious public problem

## TABLE 34

Influence of Education, Residence, Age, and Income on Willingness
to Be Taxed to Support Water Pollution Control
(N=984)
(in percent)

| Amount Willing to Be Taxed (in dollars) | Education | | | | Residence | | Age | | | Income | | | | |
|---|---|---|---|---|---|---|---|---|---|---|---|---|---|---|
| | 7 Years or less N=38 | 7-9 Years N=61 | 10-12 Years N=493 | Some College N=392 | City N=458 | Suburb N=526 | Under 40 N=482 | Above 40 N=502 | Unknown N=48 | Under $3,000 N=88 | $3,000- 7,000 N=262 | $7,000- 10,000 N=301 | $10,000- 15,000 N=209 | Above $15,000 N=78 |
| 0 | 38[b] | 36 | 23 | 11 | 17 | 24 | 12[b] | 26 | 53 | 38[b] | 24 | 14 | 13 | 16 |
| 3 | 12 | 25 | 15 | 13 | 14 | 15 | 14 | 15 | 11 | 23 | 19 | 16 | 8 | 3 |
| 5 | 12 | 14 | 22 | 15 | 17 | 15 | 19 | 15 | 11 | 8 | 22 | 21 | 14 | 10 |
| 10 | 2 | 8 | 23 | 28 | 26 | 26 | 29 | 23 | 13 | 17 | 24 | 28 | 28 | 28 |
| 15 | 0 | 4 | 5 | 9 | 8 | 8 | 7 | 8 | 3 | 2 | 3 | 7 | 15 | 13 |
| 20 | 6 | 13 | 12 | 24 | 18 | 13 | 19 | 13 | 7 | 12 | 8 | 14 | 22 | 30 |

[a]Statistically significant at the 0.01 level of confidence.
[b]Statistically significant at the 0.001 level of confidence.

122

and that public officials and institutions are seen as responsible for its control and elimination. Probably the most important finding is that persons regard water problems differently, on the basis of differing personal characteristics.

With respect to the importance of water pollution relative to other local problems, it is clear that persons of lower socioeconomic status, who are likely to live in the central city, attach less salience to this problem. The better off financially, the better educated, and the younger feel more directly affected by water pollution and place it higher in their set of policy preferences. In addition, they are more willing to be taxed for water pollution control purposes than are the less educated, the less well off, and the older.

Water pollution control emerges, then, as a middle-class issue. Costly public programs to abate pollution, such as the Pure Waters Program (a $1 billion bond and spending effort) in New York State, can be seen either as serving the preferences of those who attach high importance to water pollution over other public programs or as serving the better educated, higher income persons who tend to be suburbanites. From the evidence it is clear that those in lower socioeconomic categories, chiefly in the cities, regard other problems as more pressing. It is not to their priority preferences that public policy is responding, for it is the middle-class majorities and the relatively well-educated and well-off influentials in the state and county who have a greater impact on public policy.[3]

Still another factor is involved. Not only do middle and upper socioeconomic categories regard water pollution as a more pressing problem, but they probably also regard it as a solvable problem. If enough money and skills were made available, a technological victory over water pollution control could be achieved. Many other public problems do not lend themselves to such optimism. Certainty of means for effective treatment of housing or employment problems might result in the channeling of skills and funds in the direction of lower-status individuals, but their solutions are both more controversial and considerably less certain. There seems to be a tendency to direct skills and resources to those public problems that are less controversial and amenable to technical victory. The findings of this research, however, provide no evidence for this hypothesis; they merely suggest it.

As circumstances change, public opinion changes. The measurement and understanding of public orientations are means by which governments can gauge responses to changing conditions. It is certain that water pollution is a characteristic of an urbanized, industrialized, and growing society. As Onondaga County has grown and become more urban and industrial, the quality of its water has noticeably decreased. This research indicates that the majority of county residents are concerned about pollution and feel that government is responsible for a remedy. They also seem to feel that they can afford that remedy. The New York State Pure Waters Act and bond issue, coupled with money from the national government and county sources, will enable the county ultimately to respond to prevailing public opinion.

## CONTRASTING COGNITIONS OF THE
## POLLUTION PROBLEM

In order to analyze further the complex process of policy-making and the interaction of public opinion and policy-making, an attempt was made to compare the data with the views and perceptions of 32 knowledgeable individuals chosen for their proximity to the pollution control policy process.* The methodology adopted for this section involved the semistructured interview. While the structured interview is more precise and scientific, it was unsatisfactory for the purposes here; it was not desired to query all the respondents about the same things, nor were all the respondents competent in all the areas in which the authors were interested. The most useful method was to print an interview schedule that included the questions basic to the subject and then to ask each respondent questions suggested either by his competence or by the direction of the conversation. Thus, all the subjects were asked whether they perceived pollution as a problem in Onondaga County and how they ranked it relative to other metropolitan problems. All subjects were also asked what people and institutions they considered to be most influential in policies and matters regarding water pollution. In this way an attempt was made to establish the position of each respondent on this controversial subject at an early point in the meeting, enabling one not to exacerbate stated biases and thereby lose rapport. It was likewise possible to locate his major areas of competency and allow him to tell what he knew best.

With the consent of the respondent a small and unobtrusive portable tape recorder was used during the interview. The overwhelming majority of respondents consented to the use of the tape recorder, and only on a few occasions was there sensed some restraint on the part of the subject and the recorder turned off. It was thus possible to listen again to the whole interview and carefully take notes on the substance of the conversation. The range of people interviewed covered county and city officials directly involved in the matter of

_____

*See Table 3 for a list of individuals interviewed.

pollution policy, members of the then Board of Supervisors (now County Legislature), members of the City Council, who were also members of the public works committee, and leaders of other groups in the community seeming to have an interest in or influence on pollution matters.

Without exception all those interviewed thought that pollution is a problem in Syracuse. Great differences arose, however, when one began to define what was meant by the word "problem." There is a very clear and positive correlation between considering the problem critical and lacking broad knowledge of the overall subject. Invariably, heads of county departments directly involved with the pollution problem and engineers personally involved in major studies feel it is both necessary and desirable to take serious steps in controlling the problem, yet they do not see pollution as being so immediate and overwhelming as to transcend all other urban priorities.

For example, a prominent technical specialist on pollution in the county, who has been intimately involved in all county efforts in the past three decades and is considered by many other respondents as the man most knowledgeable about the matter, responded that, as much as he knew about the seriousness of pollution, he would say it was not as important as the blacks then rioting in Detroit. Many depreciated the seriousness of the pollution problem because they thought it mostly affected recreational activities and not the more basic need of water supply. The county currently gets its drinking water from Lakes Ontario, Skaneateles, and Otisco, none of which have, at least for the present, a critical pollution problem. Hence, the fact that fishing and swimming in Onondaga Lake have been affected does not credibly make pollution a serious metropolitan problem.

## Pollution as a Limiting Factor
### in Economic Growth

The interviewees were asked if they considered pollution a limiting factor on the economic growth of the community. The majority of people considered most knowledgeable about the economic condition of the county do not find pollution hindering growth and development. On the contrary, many notice the necessity for manufacturing industries to dispose of waste products and the need for a place to dispose of them. One then has to assess the benefits the industries bring to a region in terms of job opportunities and taxes to decide whether such benefits outweigh the admittedly deleterious effects of pollution. One has similarly to consider the costs and benefits of population growth in a region, since pollution from sanitary sewage provides a larger problem than industrial pollution. A consensus exists that pollution is not a limiting factor in the economic growth of the county. Many feel that the completion of the pipeline from Lake Ontario dispelled many of the fears of prospective industries. The recent water shortage in this area had posed the question of whether the county could provide an adequate water supply, but the new unlimited supply from Lake Ontario has convincingly answered the question in the affirmative.

Varying opinions were expressed among the economically knowledgeable over what is the most economically rational solution for Lake Onondaga. On one extreme are those who feel that the lake should be considered as an economic resource and left to be a giant cesspool, with no more money spent on it. These people feel that there are a sufficient number of nonpolluted bodies of water in the county that could be used for recreational purposes and that Onondaga Lake would be most valuable if left as a source of cheap sewage disposal for both industry and the general population. Another group, somewhat less extreme than the above, feels that a very careful study ought to be made as to the real potential of the lake. This group pointed to the fact that even in Indian times the lake was salty and of somewhat high temperature. No matter which treatment is introduced, it will still remain the place of discharge for the county's sewage effluent. Hence, these people feel that before vast sums are spent on treatment and reclamation of the lake it should be made reasonably certain that this money would not be wasted and that the improvement of the lake would be worth the costs of these projects.

A few years ago the Metropolitan Development Association, a private organization supported by local businessmen and professionals to study and make suggestions regarding the maintenance of business prosperity and opportunity in Syracuse, hired the architect Clothilde Woodward Smith to make a study of what might be done in developing the area around the lake. She came up with some very exciting and interesting proposals that showed the possibility of considerable economic fortune existed in developing recreational, resort, and housing installations in the lake area. These opportunities clearly could not materialize, however, unless reclamation made the lake both usable and appealing. Thus, the moderates feel that a careful cost-benefit analysis should be the crucial element in deciding what to do with the lake.

A rather large group in the center feels that a problem like pollution is not a matter for cost-benefit analysis. These people feel that clean water is a community value that cannot be measured by tools of economic rationality. They often reflect notions of democratic thought that such decisions should be made by the people rather than pragmatically. Many feel that the voice of the people had already been clearly heard in the 3 to 1 approval of the state's pure water program referendum.

Moving toward the opposite end of the spectrum is a more radical group, described as those with a conservationist bent. This group feels that there is great economic utility in solving the pollution problem, but in the last analysis their conservationist values are the basis for their feelings. One typical person in this group noted the incompetence of the present leadership in the antipollution area. He suggested that the present program to provide secondary treatment is foolish, since without some form of additional treatment a terrible algae problem would result. Others in this group lauded the importance of maintaining wetlands and sanctuaries for animals and fish. Some voiced the opinion that the community has the responsibility to return water to its lake in the same pure condition that it takes the water, whatever the cost of this operation.

Reaching the opposite end of the spectrum are a few who feel that pollution is a limiting factor in the economic growth of the community. One interviewee in this group cited a company in town that manufactures surgical supplies requiring steel of very high quality. Until now it has been purchasing its steel from a local steel industry, but it may soon have to discontinue these purchases because the polluted lake water the local company uses is affecting the quality of the steel produced.

Thus, if one outlines the range of opinions on the matter of whether pollution is a problem in Syracuse, the following results:

1. At the top are those one might call the pragmatists. All of these people see pollution as a problem but differ as to the most rational solution. They all similarly favor some form of cost-benefit analysis in solving the problem.

2. In the middle are those who might be called the democrats. These people feel that pollution, as all other matters of community interest, ought to be left up to the people who are most directly concerned and affected. They do not necessarily suggest that referendums should decide the matter, but they do imply that the elected politicians have many indicators of public opinion and should be guided by the will of the people rather than merely by economic rationality. This group does not tend to be as knowledgeable as the pragmatists but does demonstrate a relative awareness of the problem. More members of this group favor constructing additional facilities, since they feel the people want them, but many are against it, noting that it would increase taxes against the people's wishes.

3. On the bottom are the conservationists with a few pragmatists filling out the picture. The conservationists typically overlook costs and the will of the people and are most interested in preserving nature in a virgin condition. The exceptional pragmatists see the cost-benefit equation as implying a massive attack on pollution.

## Pollution in a Range of Priorities

The other question that all the respondents were asked was how they would rank water pollution against other urban problems in Onondaga County. Only two individuals see water pollution as the number one urban problem. One of them ought to be taken seriously, since he has been very vocal about this opinion and has strong conservationist feelings, as indicated by his involvement in the sporting business. The other individual may be taken somewhat less seriously because of his consistently demonstrated flair for the dramatic. This individual is an expert on various aspects of pollution in the community and is also the most vocal and active critic of the county's lethargy and lack of interest in reclaiming Onondaga Lake. In a rather long interview he repeatedly showed knowledge of and sensitivity to the many urban problems facing the community and the scarcity of funds for all of them, yet he stubbornly reiterated his ranking of pollution as number one. Since he has spent so much of his time and effort in an individual campaign to educate the community and its leadership to the pollution problem, it seems that his ranking reflects more his desire not to denigrate his great efforts in this campaign rather than his considered appraisal of urban priorities.

Among the overwhelming majority who do not see pollution as the major urban problem, there still exist great variations as to how the members rank pollution. Again, there is a correlation between knowing more about the problem and ranking it lower on the urban priority list. A ranking official in the Division of Drainage and Sanitation responded that the people lately have been active in applying pressure in regard to water pollution. He feels that this vigorous public interest outweighs the pressing nature of the problem in demanding an increase in antipollution facilities. A very influential engineer long associated with efforts to install treatment facilities in the county reiterated how central the matter of available funds is to the urban priority schedule. If the county had unlimited funds it could completely eliminate the problem of pollution in the shortest possible time. He continued, however, and noted that, since funds are so scarce, the county cannot recklessly channel too much into an area less immediately threatening than other urban problems such as poverty. A prominent member of the Board of Supervisors who would be extremely influential in the allocation of funds for new antipollution facilities feels that additional treatment facilities should be a very low priority item as long as millions of gallons of untreated sewage keep flowing into the lake from storm overflow.

A high official in the county's Board of Health noted that, since pollution is not currently a problem affecting health or contributing to sickness in the county, it should not be considered as taking precedence over many other urban problems that do threaten the well-being of the community. Another influential member of the Board of Supervisors noted that mandated programs must be taken care of first. Medicaid must be paid for immediately. Roads and other public facilities must operate effectively now. Pollution expenditures, he concluded, have to defer to these more immediate necessities. A high level Public Works official noted that pollution cannot be considered a high priority item, since so many steps are being taken to contain it. Pollution, he continued, is not a problem in which a large sum of money spent today completely eliminates the problem. Pollution is an ongoing problem that is constantly changing with growths of population and changes in the industrial population of the county. Consequently, it can never be solved, for new reactions will always be necessary to treat additional types of pollutants that are fed into the sewage. Hence, keeping pollution at a tolerable level is about the best a growing industrial county can do.

Although there is a correlation between greater knowledge of the pollution problem and the cognition of its lower priority as a metropolitan problem, the authors are in no way implying that there is any definitive evidence that demands the conclusion that pollution is not a high priority problem for the county. The presence of this correlation can probably be explained best by the fact that the preponderance of the interviewees are politicians actively involved in the process of trying to find funds in the limited county budget for all the pressing problems of a metropolitan area. Since the available funds fall so short of current needs it is often the unfortunate condition that the threat of an imminent crisis is what determines the allocation of funds. It is not surprising, therefore, that the more knowledgeable of the respondents are likewise most aware that pollution, while threatening to become critical in the near future, is not immediately critical, and they thus postpone for the present time allocating the scarce county funds. Although this kind of muddling through is inevitably self-defeating, it is nevertheless usually the choice made by politicians faced with limited funds, growing problems, and great resistance to constantly rising taxes.

# 9

## THE INDIVIDUAL
## IN THE POLICY PROCESS

The dynamism of the policy process can be seen through an analysis of the role and impact of individual personalities. In addition to an understanding of the complex interactions among leadership components and between them and public opinion, the interviews with political influentials provide a view of patterns of leadership, specialized rules, and motivation.

The study of personal influence and the role of the individual has had a very intriguing history and has been the source of great debate in the social sciences. Max Weber has analyzed the role of the individual in society and has coined the term "charisma" to describe the phenomenon of great personal influence over a substantial number of people. Weber is convinced that certain types of polities are completely dominated and ruled on the basis of charismatic leadership. Historians have long pondered whether great people create destiny or destiny enlists great people to fulfill its tasks. This study has no pretensions to a dramatic solution of this historical debate. The following pages merely reflect the bias that, above and beyond the demonstrated importance of the organizational basis of government, there are on occasion individuals whose personalities have a powerful impact on public policy. Such personalities are not limited to institutional roles. They may be found among interested citizens as well.

### THE COUNTY EXECUTIVE

The respondents were asked whom they considered to be the influential decision-makers in pollution matters. The person who received the most acknowledgment is, not surprisingly, John Mulroy, the county executive. The deputy county executive sees Mulroy as the most influential person in any governmental decision, since he must recommend any major new policy before the Board of Supervisors can make approvals and appropriations. The commissioner of public works likewise sees the county executive as the person with most influence in water pollution policy. As shown in Table 35, 22 out of 29 respondents mentioned Mulroy among the people they consider most influential in pollution decision-making.

Closely following Mulroy with 17 acknowledgments each are Uhl Mann and John Hennigan, heads of the Division of Drainage and Sanitation. Commenting on his subordinates, the commissioner of public works considered Mann and Hennigan to be highly informed in matters of water pollution. For many years the Division of Drainage and Sanitation has constructed and operated most of the county's treatment facilities in addition to taking water samples. The deputy county executive feels that Mann and Hennigan would therefore easily carry the most weight in regard to innovations and new policies in the area of water pollution. Many respondents are aware that Uhl Mann is an outstanding authority in the field of sewage treatment and disposal and realize that a comparatively small county like Onondaga is fortunate in having been able to attract a man of his stature. Both Hennigan and Mann are viewed as experts, bringing to pollution policy competent consideration of alternatives and rational selection of final policy. Respondents noted that both men have attended conferences and seminars on pollution throughout the country in order to keep abreast of latest findings and techniques, a fact that contributes to the influence of their recommendations with the executive and the Board of Supervisors.

The person regarded as third in influence is Daniel Jackson, with 17 votes. Jackson is a member of Syracuse University's engineering department and specializes in limnology. For a number of years he has been running almost a one-man crusade to initiate a reclamation program for Onondaga Lake. He recently acquired the use of a moderate-size vessel that he turned into a laboratory for studying the condition of the lake. In the summer of 1967 Jackson unfolded what he called Project '70, a detailed program for reclamation of the lake, to be financed by a bond issue. Jackson also campaigns through mass media and has received an enormous amount of coverage.

The respondents who acknowledge Jackson's influence see it mainly as indirect. Jackson's role is viewed largely as attracting public opinion and providing good ideas that may interest those more directly involved in the decision-making process. It is in this respect that the deputy county executive considers Jackson to be influential. Only recently, he noted, the county executive lunched with Jackson to discuss one of his current programs. An official in Drainage and

TABLE 35

Influential Persons in Pollution Decision-Making*

| Person | Number of Times Mentioned |
|---|---|
| John Mulroy | 22 |
| Uhl Mann and John Hennigan | 17 |
| Daniel Jackson | 17 |
| Earl O'Brien | 14 |
| Commissioner David Bigwood | 12 |
| William Walsh | 8 |
| Senator John Hughes | 6 |
| Thad Collum | 5 |
| Lyle Hornbeck | 5 |
| Commissioner Edwin M. Baylard | 4 |
| Ephraim Schapero | 3 |
| James Hanley | 2 |
| Elmer Bogardus | 2 |
| Fred Keith | 2 |
| Commissioner John Meixell | 2 |
| Senator Robert Kennedy | 1 |
| Calvin Hamilton | 1 |
| Thomas Dyer | 1 |
| John Searles | 1 |
| James Hancock, Jr. | 1 |
| Peter Guola | 1 |
| Millard Rogers | 1 |
| George Schuster | 1 |
| Nelson L. Nemerow | 1 |
| Nyrton C. Rand | 1 |

*A perfect score would have been 29, the total number of people who responded to this question. Each vote represents acknowledgement by one interviewee that the said person is influential in pollution decision-making.

Sanitation commented that Jackson had the blessings of the newspapers, which do much to instill opinions in the public. "I don't think Jackson could pressure the county into adopting his 'Project '70,'" the deputy county executive continued, "but I think the newspapers can." The commissioner of public works also acknowledges Jackson's influence on pollution matters. The commissioner feels that Jackson is, quite wisely, being taken seriously in county government. A Republican official credits Jackson with stimulating many existing pollution policies in the county. Also among respondents receptive to Jackson's work is the majority leader of the Board of Supervisors, who agrees that Jackson's opinions are to be taken seriously.

## AN INFLUENTIAL FROM THE PROFESSIONS

Earl O'Brien, with 14 acknowledgements, is the fourth most frequently named individual having influence on pollution matters. Most of the people who acknowledge O'Brien are older politicians who probably associate him with pollution activities of the past. One reason for O'Brien's high score may be that the firm that bears his name is still deeply involved in pollution studies and construction of facilities, although O'Brien has been taking a lesser role in the business lately. One Division of Drainage and Sanitation official noted that O'Brien was influential in establishing the Metropolitan Treatment Plant. Since then, however, he has not been responsible for any major proposal. The deputy county executive credits O'Brien's influence to his background as an engineer and his great prestige among county officials. This official, however, does not think that the executive would rely on O'Brien personally but would rather acknowledge reports of his firm.

On the other hand, an aging yet extremely influential lawyer who has held formal government positions and has enjoyed a long association informally within high government and Republican Party circles feels that Earl O'Brien would be one of the principal factors in policies dealing with pollution in the county. Because of his knowledge and initiative, the respondent continued, nontechnical people in government rely on O'Brien. Similarly, another older party official noted that over a long period O'Brien has made reliable studies for the county. Because of his thoroughness and accuracy he commands great respect and confidence. In perspective, it seems that O'Brien was an extremely influential force in pollution matters for a very long time but that in the most recent period, possibly because of his semiretirement, his influence and involvement have waned considerably. His firm, nevertheless, remains active in pollution programs to this day.

The next highest number of acknowledgements is 12 for Commissioner David Bigwood of the Health Department. The important role played by the County Health Department has been mentioned many times in this book, and it is fitting that the respondents agree on the importance of its role. The reason Commissioner Bigwood's score is somewhat less than other of the important participants may be that his department was relatively young, only about six months old, at the time this study was made.

## THE MAYOR OF SYRACUSE

The mayor of the city of Syracuse, William Walsh, received 8 acknowledgments, indicating an important role in pollution decision-making, although the problem falls under county jurisdiction. Walsh is responsible for the intercepting sewer system in the city of Syracuse and for its operational success. Earlier, the problem of the city's interceptor sewers and their responsibility for millions of gallons of raw sewage that flow into the lake following heavy rainfalls was assessed. The city corporation counsel stated that 11 companies feed raw sewage into Onondaga Creek and that the city must bear responsibility for correcting this situation. The corporation counsel noted also that the cleaning and replacement of interceptor sewers are the responsibilities of the mayor of Syracuse as well. A lawyer who has held city government posts in the past noted that the mayor would be a vital participant in pollution programs since the city must bear the cost of a large part of these programs.

The remaining people who receive token acknowledgment are involved in a particular decision occasionally but can hardly be considered among the major pollution decision-makers. One person, however, provides an important perspective on decision-making in the county.

## AN INFLUENTIAL FROM THE PARTIES

He is Thad Collum, county chairman of the Republican Party, who received 5 acknowledgments. It is likely that mention of him is symbolic of the Republican Party's predominance in Onondaga County. As a former chairman of the Board of Supervisors mentioned, the fact that the mayor and the county executive are two of the primary leaders of the Republican Party makes it clear that the party is in a dominating position in county and city government. Many of the people surveyed noted that the Republican Party is well aware of its unusual fortune in controlling the central city as well as the suburban sections of the Syracuse metropolitan area. Consequently, in order to prevent the Democratic Party from acquiring a dramatic issue, the party is particularly sensitive to policies that have potential to generate wide public concern. The respondents feel that if the Republican Party is outspoken on a particular issue it will prevail, but in the majority of cases party officials do not interfere with the policy-making operations of elected leaders. Hence, the party very naturally restricts its involvement to the largest policy questions, particularly those that, if neglected, would endanger the future success of the

Republicans at the polls. In an area as technical as water pollution the respondents thought it unlikely that the Republican Party would become involved unless it concerned a tax increase to finance the program.

## EXTERNAL INFLUENCE

The final question posed concerned the importance of the federal and state governments on pollution matters in Onondaga County. In the latter part of Chapter 6 the effect of federal and state funds on the construction of local treatment facilities was traced. It was noted there that the federal government's removal of a maximum limitation on the size of individual grants and the state's passage of the Pure Waters Act greatly increased the number of antipollution treatment facilities constructed in the county. It was similarly noted that in the first year following the pure waters program the county received from the federal and state governments four times the total amount it had received in the preceding decade. Similarly, with the expected approval of applications made in 1967, the county will have received a full ten times more in aid in 1966 and 1967 than in the decade 1955-65.

Almost all of the respondents, whether in the legislative branch, the executive branch, or the private sector, agreed that the stimulus from the federal and state governments is very important. The majority leader of the Board of Supervisors felt the state has been overwhelmingly responsible for the current mandate to impose secondary treatment. "I doubt," he said, "that the county would have adopted secondary treatment on its own, nor could we have afforded this without federal and state aid."

A state senator from Syracuse noted that the major inhibitor of large-scale projects to end pollution in this county is an economic one. Without state and federal support, he continued, the county would not have built most of the facilities that presently combat pollution. A member of the Syracuse Common Council said that nothing is really accomplished in the county in matters of water pollution without impetus and financial help from the state and federal governments. By contrast, a member of the Board of Supervisors felt that the county would have been building treatment facilities even without state and federal aid. He admitted, however, that it would have been building the cheapest facilities possible. The impetus from the state and federal government, he continued, can be seen from the fact that the county is now adopting secondary treatment, which it would not have done independently.

Respondents from the executive branch are particularly aware of the impact of external influence. The commissioner of public works sees the involvement of the state and federal governments as critically important for the success of pollution abatement in Onondaga County. Previously, industries that polluted the waters threatened to leave whenever local authorities attempted to control the pollution. Now, he stated, the state and federal governments set standards and time limits that industry must meet. Without federal and state impetus, Onondaga County would have been unable to enforce the controls or build the facilities that are presently in operation. The County Health Department dispenses state funds and thus must comply with state policies, as it must comply with federal policies when it dispenses federal funds. The Health Department's head of environmental engineering noted that the federal and state governments provide two-thirds of the cost of new antipollution facilities. Furthermore, he continued, the state now pays one-third of the annual cost of operations and maintenance of local treatment plants. In the event that a locality resists making expenditures for some new facility deemed necessary, the state can withdraw the 33 percent maintenance reimbursement. With the rising costs of maintaining facilities, this 33 percent reimbursement is a firm lever to ensure compliance with state policies.

A Division of Drainage and Sanitation official noted that the state has effectively advanced the adoption of secondary treatment and single facilities for multiple localities. The state promotes its policy of fewer and larger facilities for large areas by not approving applications for smaller plants, thus denying funds needed for their construction. A well-known member of the Republican Party concurred that federal and state impetus in this manner has greatly furthered the county's antipollution program. An elderly and influential lawyer and banker reminisced of the 1940s, when the Onondaga County Reclamation Association, which he formerly headed, recognized the state's potential power in antipollution activities and consequently focused its attack on the state.

The survey reveals overwhelming agreement that the federal and state governments have been extremely influential in making local governments aware of and responsive to antipollution programs. Currently, they share the responsibility for continuing and increasing the sophistication of local antipollution efforts. There is consensus as well that the primary impact of the federal and state role is in providing funds for the construction of facilities. Respondents agree that recognition of the pollution problem and efforts to solve it existed during the entire postwar period and that independent local efforts were made prior to the great national awareness of the problem. One may conclude that local awareness was primarily responsible for the county's taking full advantage of federal and state funds when they became available. It was, of course, the large amount of external funds that allowed the county to develop the extensive facilities system that it presently has and is still building. Furthermore, there is consensus that the current investigation of possible tertiary treatment has been likewise spurred by the federal and state governments.

## INSTITUTIONAL INFLUENCE
## IN THE POLICY PROCESS

The next question posed to the respondents regarded the governmental agencies they considered most responsible in handling matters of pollution. Obviously, this was an attempt to determine through this question the agencies directly involved in pollution policy matters and the relative importance ascribed the various agencies by politicians most closely connected to the decision-making process. It might be inferred from an approach of this type that certain agencies are solely responsible for decision-making and policy formation. This would be in direct contradiction to the "systems" view of the political process, which suggests a continual interaction of various levels of input and output as the environment from which policy derives. The authors concur with this dynamic view of the decision-making process, as has been made clear throughout these pages. In the approach here the various agencies involved in the overall process are merely defined; it is not being suggested that decisions are made by these agencies in isolation from other political forces, although, as suggested, such forces have assumed a great deal of importance in the political process.

## THE COUNTY EXECUTIVE

The unit of government considered to be most influential in matters of water pollution by the overwhelming majority of the respondents is the county executive. Considering the trend of executive dominance in Western countries, this view would not seem surprising if it were not for the fact that the office of county executive is only a few years old. Up until a few years ago the major population concentration in Onondaga County was in the city of Syracuse. Consequently, most major policy matters affecting the county were in the

hands of the city government, with the County Board of Supervisors
the major governmental unit for those areas under county jurisdiction.
Following the postwar exodus from the central city to the suburbs,
the noncity population of the county has been growing at a faster rate
than the central city population, and in the past few years the noncity
population has finally surpassed that of the city of Syracuse. With
this rapid growth of county population the demands on county government clearly began to surpass the limited ability of the Board of
Supervisors, and therefore it was decided to institute a county executive. Since its inception in 1962 the office of county executive has
dramatically grown both in power and breadth of jurisdiction. Last
year the county executive issued a call for a 2 percent increase in
sales tax in stark opposition to the stated opinion of Republican Party
influentials such as Thad Collum. It is a testimony to the growth in
status of the county executive that he prevailed and the party reversed
itself.

## THE BOARD OF SUPERVISORS

The great influence of the county executive comes from the
fact that the Board of Supervisors, like the preponderance of Western
legislatures, is inadequate in both size and expertise to originate the
amount of legislation it is required to pass. Hence, the Board is
quite dependent on the executive branch to make recommendations,
which it then considers as extensively or superficially as it wishes.
The county executive is in turn greatly dependent on the various
departments under his jurisdiction to provide him with the qualified
staff needed to research and formulate the programs that are eventually presented to the Board of Supervisors for their approval. It
must be remembered, however, that the county executive cannot
generate funds on his own and is, in the last analysis, dependent on
the Board of Supervisors to allocate the funds necessary to support
his programs.

Before its replacement on January 1, 1968, by the Onondaga
County Legislature, the Onondaga County Board of Supervisors was
the legislative unit for the county. A far cry from the traditional
conception of organizations always trying to increase their size and
function, the Board of Supervisors remained a very conservative body,
even resisting the efforts to give it the greater powers that inevitably
arose with the marked growth of the county. Its membership com-
prised a total of 38 supervisors, with 19 representing the towns in
the county. The Board of Supervisors has never been accused of being
a dynamic body, and in the past it has very often been described as
merely carrying out the wishes of the Republican Party. In recent

years, however, with the growth in county size and governmental complexity the traditional monolithic view of the county has become increasingly inaccurate.[1] Although the Board of Supervisors has certainly not turned into a dynamic body, it has become much more independent than it was during the hegemony of Rolland Marvin and Stuart Hancock over the party. In matters of water pollution the Board has a very important role since, in the last analysis, it is the only source of funds. Programs and policies are developed and initiated elsewhere for the most part, but if they need a financial outlay the Board is pivotal for final adoption of the program.

As a very influential engineer long associated with pollution programs stated, the county executive, as administrative head of the county, has certain responsibilities, but he can carry out his responsibilities only if he is given the necessary funds. He doesn't have the power to levy taxes. Rather, to provide money for his programs, he submits a budget to the Board of Supervisors, who approve it, reject it, or change it. The county executive develops programs, makes recommendations, and provides expert testimony. He may be in a position to exercise more influence on the Board of Supervisors than any other person, but he certainly cannot control the Board. Programs and policies regarding water pollution, after they have been developed and discussed elsewhere, go to the Committee of Public Works of the Board of Supervisors. The Committee then makes its own investigation of the program and votes on it. Approval by the Committee is tantamount to approval by the Board.

The various county departments become important participants in the decision-making process when their areas of specialty are required in formulating the program in question. To a great extent, the scope of their involvement will depend on the initiative of the particular administrative agency. The agency may respond merely to directions and initiatives emanating from the executive or may take a more active role in planning and researching for exigencies that arise. The influence of the agency or department will be greatly enhanced if it sees its role as an innovator and continually provides the executive with suggestions for new programs and policies.

## THE DIVISION OF DRAINAGE AND SANITATION

One of the agencies most closely involved with pollution is the Division of Drainage and Sanitation, which is part of the County Public Works Commission. The perceptions of the respondents regarding the influence of the Division vary greatly. Some believe it is highly innovative and influential, while others think it is passive and of marginal influence. A high Republican Party official considers the Division of Drainage and Sanitation as very involved with pollution matters, but mainly in carrying out the directions of the elected officials. The county executive, he continues, leans heavily on the technical expertise and suggestions of the Division but decides on final policy himself. A high official on the legal staff considers the Division as the agency most involved in water pollution matters. Of course, he noted, it does not make decisions that commit the county to a policy direction or that involve expenditures of money. Rather, the Division reviews policies in detail and develops solutions that must then be approved at higher levels. The head of a very influential engineering firm that has worked for the county in building its anti-pollution facilities sees the Division as mainly an operating agency carrying out measures and instructions that are given to it and for which money is provided. A professor who is a very vocal critic of the county pollution policies sees no governmental agency as really active in water pollution matters. The Division is helpful, he says, but not to any large extent.

On the other hand, a large number of people intimately involved in matters relating to pollution see the Division of Drainage and Sanitation as having a very influential and innovative role in pollution policy. The deputy county executive sees the Division as carrying the most weight in innovation and new policies. A former chairman of the Board of Supervisors, presently a consultant for a county agency, sees policy emanating from the Division, since it is in the best position to notice developments in pollution requirements and needs and consequently to make the necessary plans and recommendations. The Syracuse city engineer, who has jurisdiction for the interceptor sewers in the city and who is also a member of the county's governmental committee on Onondaga Lake, states that the Division makes most recommendations to the Board of Supervisors and the county executive on policy matters. When an official in the Division of Drainage and Sanitation was asked how influential he considered his agency to be, he noted that the Division has had no trouble in getting its measures through the Board and that the Board normally fulfills the Division's requests for funds.

The disparate opinions regarding the influence of the Division of Drainage and Sanitation can be understood somewhat by recalling the systems model alluded to above. Clearly, both groups of respondents were close to the situation, yet one group saw a devolution of policy from below to above. It is difficult to measure which is the more significant force in this policy-making process—the executive in eliciting his department to construct and delimit programs to put his broad policy into operation or the Division in providing ideas and programs for the executive to construct his policy. It is likely that both levels share in initiating the process. What is most clear, however, is that the entire process is dynamic, involving interaction of multiple sectors from both within and without government.


## THE HEALTH DEPARTMENTS

The next agency examined that has a very important role in matters of water pollution is the County Health Department. Until quite recently the State Health Department maintained a branch office in Syracuse. For the past two years, however, a new County Health Department has been established that has taken over most of the roles formerly under the jurisdiction of the state's branch office. The formal roles of the Health Department in matters of pollution are very important and have elicited intensive critical analysis from many of the respondents. The present role of the Health Department was initiated in 1949 with the passage of the state's Water Pollution Control Act (Article 12 of the Public Health Law). The bill created the Water Pollution Control Board, which consists of the heads of the departments of Conservation, Public Works, Commerce, and Agriculture and Markets, with the state health commissioner serving as chairman.[2]

The Board was assigned by the bill to maintain reasonable standards of purity for the waters of the state, consistent with the interests of public health, public enjoyment of waters, protection and propagation of fish and wildlife, and industrial development of the state. It is likewise given duties, including stimulation of voluntary cooperation to prevent or abate water pollution, encouragement of joint action in solution of problems, cooperation with other states and the federal government on pollution control matters, stimulation of research and development of comprehensive programs for pollution abatement, submission and approval of plans for sewage and waste disposal systems, and, finally, classification and adoption of quality standards for all waters of the state.[3] Perhaps the most significant role of the Board is the power of enforcement to ensure that municipalities and citizens abide by the provisions of the law. If necessary, the Board could go to court to force adherence to provisions of the pollution law.

It seems from this cursory appraisal of the Board that it could be a potent force in pollution abatement. Unfortunately, however, various loopholes in the law and the Board's image of its role have greatly diminished its effectiveness. Any party served with an order to take certain steps to abate pollution is able to obtain some delays before positive steps can be taken to force adherence. The Board has usually been satisified if a municipality or industry undertakes a progressive program to solve its pollution problem, even if the program takes many years. Thus, in the 15 years between establishment of the Board and passage of the Pure Waters Act, only very limited progress in the elimination of pollution in the state's waters was made, despite the Board's impressive formal powers. In 1963 the Board was abolished and its power given to the Water Resources Commission.

The respondents, with scant exception, take a dim view of the activity of the Board and of its representatives in the Syracuse region. They take a similarly dim view of the State Health Department, which, through its Division of Environmental Health Service, is for all practical purposes the agency that currently enforces pollution policy in the county. The deputy county executive feels that the State Health Department could be very effective in the pollution area except for the manner in which it has applied powers of enforcement. Many political and administrative ramifications have in the past precluded the effectiveness of the State Health Department. As the County Health Department grows, he feels, it should develop a strong role in matters of enforcement. It is the opinion of a high official in the Division of Drainage and Sanitation that the State Health Department was ineffective in matters of pollution for over 50 years until the advent of the Pure Waters Act. This same official feels that, once the County Health Department becomes organized, it will have quite a role, but it is currently only a few months old.

A former chairman of the Board of Supervisors perceptively suggests that the County Health Department is in the process of formulating a county health code to supplant the State Health Code, which at present has jurisdiction in the county. With these codes county health officials will be able to act in pollution matters much more effectively than the state was able to do, since the new code will conform more closely to specific county problems and needs in terms of policing pollution nuisances. A former supervisor who is a vocal critic of polluted conditions in the county sees the State Health Department as one of the most sterile groups in government. It has issued orders, he notes, that secondary treatment will increase the amount of algae in the lake to such an extent that the algae will become a severe problem.

What emerges very clearly is that in the past the State Health Department and the Water Pollution Control Board have had tremendous potential power, which is now in the hands of the County Health Department and State Water Resources Commission. Simply by changing the classification of a body of water from industrial usage to fishing, swimming, or drinking, the state can make the building of treatment facilities a necessity. Legally, the County Health Department can totally remove all pollution from this county merely by invoking existing laws. The great problem, however, is a monetary one. With unlimited funds, pollution could indeed be entirely removed. Unfortunately, local government has only limited funds, and many industries would go out of business if forced to build sufficient facilities to treat their effluent. This state of affairs explains the laxity of pollution enforcement prior to the Pure Waters Act. With the tremendous amount of funds made available through the Pure Waters Bond Issue, it has finally become possible to deal with the pollution problem and to overcome it in some areas. Through these new state and federal funds, county treatment facilities will be upgraded to secondary treatment. Also, a study is currently underway to analyze possible introduction of some form of tertiary treatment.

## OTHER AGENCIES

The next units of government in this examination are the Governmental Committee on Onondaga Lake and the Public Works Advisory Board. The Governmental Committee, created by the county executive, includes a number of heads of county departments having interests related to matters of pollution, as well as members of city government, such as the city engineer. The Committee studies proposals brought to its attention and makes recommendations to the county executive and the Board of Supervisors. The role of the Governmental Committee is that of a consultant whose opinions are respected. It does not normally originate programs or policies. For instance, the application for a federal grant to make Onondaga Lake a demonstration lake was recently sent to the Governmental Committee, which studied the proposal and then made recommendations to the Committee of Public Works of the Board of Supervisors and to the county executive. The Committee also recently studied the plans for the new secondary treatment project and sent on its approval and recommendations.

The Public Works Advisory Board is a formal governmental unit established by the county charter (section 1105) and appointed by the county executive. Presently there are nine members on the Board, all of whom are private citizens. The Board is not acknowledged as providing any expert technical advice but is seen as a means of organizing community support for certain projects and policies. Although the charter does not require that these people be private members of the community, the county executive has been inclined toward appointing private citizens, who, he feels, have a stronger link with the community.

## PRIVATE GROUPS

### The Press

Invariably, the respondents feel that the two newspapers in Syracuse have an important effect on government officials both directly and indirectly through their effect on public opinion. Not surprisingly, the elected officials, especially supervisors, are most vocal in ascribing an influential role to the news media.

A supervisor who has recently been a candidate for a county office expressed the view that elected officials are very sensitive to criticism from the newspapers; if they see a good idea given coverage by the papers they will usually pick it up. He feels that many local politicians are currently jumping on the antipollution bandwagon because it is receiving much coverage and advocacy from the press. An influential banker and lawyer in the community feels that the newspapers have an important effect on government decision-making as well. The reason newspapers have been more restrained about water pollution than they were about the Ontario water pipeline, he suggests, is probably that Samuel I. Newhouse (the owner of the city papers) does not want to buck the administration from which he stands to profit handsomely on urban renewal in the near future.

A former chairman of the Board of Supervisors feels that the newspapers in the county have demonstrated their influence time and again. Recently they showed their power in getting the vote for the referendum to go to Lake Ontario for water. This interviewee also feels that the papers were very responsible in defeating Charlie Schoeneck, a prominent Republican, and in electing Jim Hanley to the House of Representatives. An engineer long associated with pollution projects in the county feels that, although the newspapers are undoubtedly influential, they often dilute their credibility by backing contradictory programs. Very recently the Herald-Journal was complaining about a tax increase. A short time afterward, the Post-Standard, a relative of the Herald-Journal, began to talk of spending several million dollars to reclaim Onondaga Lake. How can the county both keep taxes lowered and increase the spending at the same time? One official in the Division of Drainage and Sanitation stated that if the papers would get behind a comprehensive program for attacking pollution the county could be pressured into adopting it. The deputy county executive feels that, although no definite plan to eliminate pollution in the county has been adopted, the newspapers will expedite any attack on pollution by continually keeping the problem before the people and the politicians.

Clearly, none of the respondents overlooks the influence of the newspapers on county government. There is some disagreement as to how effectively this nebulous influence is translated into effective pressure on particular policies. Few, however, question the great impact of the papers when they back specific programs.

### Industrial and Business Groups

Industrial and business groups are also a very important element to examine for an understanding of pollution decision-making in the county. In looking at this category of groups, it is worthwhile to make a clear demarcation between activities of these groups in the past and their activities in the most recent years, during which public opinion has expressed, rather clearly, its desire to combat water pollution. Industrial concerns have been among the leading contributors to the pollution problem of Onondaga County for a long time. Industries on the shores of Onondaga Lake feed pollutants directly into its waters. Many more plants throughout the county empty pollutants into the sewage, which similarly enter the lake. These same industries are also a source of great economic wealth for the county. They provide income to a great number of county residents and purchase products and services locally. It is this symbiotic relationship with the community that has enabled these industries to avoid the tremendous costs of treating their effluents and removing pollutants for so long.

It is only natural for industries to avoid great expense, and it is likewise natural for people economically dependent upon them to accommodate their desire to avoid these expenses. An aging banker and lawyer long associated with pollution projects described a variety of incidents in which he witnessed the large industries interfering with efforts at pollution control. Large local industries, he said, had in their corner the powerful railroads that shipped their products, helping to quell any antipollution interference with their operations. He reminisced further about the time in the late 1940s when a number of private groups were led by the Junior Chamber of Commerce in a drive to enlist vast support for an antipollution program. The large industries, who were prime contributors to the Junior Chamber of Commerce, interfered.

A reporter on one of the city's two major newspapers who has specialized in the pollution problem noted that Crucible Steel closes its plant every year at the time that the adjacent state fair is being operated. If it remained in operation, the smoke from the Crucible plant would be a great nuisance and would keep people away from the fair. Consequently, the not surprising arrangement between Crucible and the state is that if Crucible closes down for the fair, the state will not bother Crucible about its pollution.

One Republican Party official, who might have been expected to be a little reticent, since large industry is among his party's chief supporters, readily admitted that the large industries have retarded the development of antipollution measures because of obvious self-interest. There is overwhelming agreement among the respondents that the industries in the county have been blatantly feeding their pollutants into the lake for years without the slightest thought to avoiding widescale pollution.

The past decade has witnessed widespread recognition in both government and the private sector that water pollution is rapidly reaching critical proportions. In an earlier section the many federal and state bills that have been passed in an effort to halt water pollution were traced. What has come to serve as a watershed in New York State activities is the often-mentioned Pure Waters Act, approved by a convincing 3:1 ratio by the voters in the state. The Act supplied the money, and the state immediately responded to this clear mandate by requiring secondary treatment facilities throughout the state. The countless industries and businesses involved in pollution practices had been following these federal and state developments very closely; they quickly realized that if they did not become directly involved in the growing antipollution movement the whole thrust of the movement would be turned upon them. Hence, in Onondaga County one finds the local Manufacturers' Association forming a special committee on water and air pollution, the Metropolitan Development Association, commissioning a wide study of the economic effects of pollution, and, even more significantly, the major delinquent industries beginning to study the problem and cooperating with governmental efforts to attack the pollution problem in the county.

The significance of this new policy of cooperation cannot be overestimated. One clear example of the importance of industry and business in clearing up pollution can be observed in some recent activities of the Manufacturers' Association. Recently, the county submitted an application for a grant from the federal government to make Onondaga Lake a demonstration lake to test the effectiveness of a cooperative program between federal and local government and private industry in attacking water pollution. The Manufacturers' Association cooperated with Health and Public Works authorities in assembling the information necessary for making this application. The Association sent out surveys to its members asking for various facts needed by the county and state authorities. The Association also cooperated in enabling county authorities to visit its member plants to study their effluent in order to know what treatment is necessary to neutralize the various pollutants discharged by local industries.

Individual industries are also engaging their staffs and funds in studying how to combat pollution most effectively in the county. Solvay Process is engaged with the county in a cooperative effort to study a combined treatment system involving county facilities and Solvay facilities. This system may enable Solvay to provide the mandated secondary treatment to its effluent and provide some form of tertiary treatment for the county sewage as well. In studying the lake, Solvay has also discovered that there is a high quality limestone at the bottom of the lake beneath about six feet of waste. This discovery may provide an economic stimulus that would expedite dredging the bottom of the lake.

Any altruistic intent on the part of industry is not implied here, nor is it being denied. It is, however, being suggested that the recent cooperative attitude on the part of industry and its professional organizations is the result of the dynamic interaction of a multitude of governmental and nongovernmental forces. Clearly, Solvay's cooperation with the county on a tertiary facility will enable Solvay to get federal funds that it would not be able to receive if it constructed its secondary treatment facility alone. Without the overwhelming vote on the Pure Waters Act, the state would probably never have mandated secondary treatment. Without the availability of federal funds, which state and local government are eager to take advantage of, the state Pure Waters Act would probably never have been conceived. These are only a few of the forces that have combined to reverse the attitude of industry.

A matter of great interest to this study was how influential the respondents considered the various industrial and business groups to be in pollution decision-making in the county. There was general agreement among those closest to the scene that these industrial and business groups would not be involved at all except if the group desired to make contact with the government. The deputy county executive did not think the executive would contact groups such as the Manufacturers' Association on matters of pollution policy except to get certain facts and information. These groups might, however, contact him if they felt some policy affected them. The commissioner of public works likewise felt that these groups would never be involved in policy-making but would be involved in matters affecting their members and for which cooperation on the part of their members was desirable. There was also agreement that these groups would not hesitate to make their views known to party officials, as well as government officials, when a policy greatly affected them. There was also feeling that the one group that takes a little more objective approach to pollution matters is the Metropolitan Development Association (MDA) and that should a comprehensive program to eliminate pollution be embarked upon, it is likely that the MDA might be the coordinating body.

There is considerable agreement among higher officials directly involved in policy formation that influence accrues to these business groups because they represent an influential sector of the county. When government embarks upon large programs, it recognizes the wisdom of enlisting as many sectors in support of the programs as can possibly be found. The commissioner of public works notes that public endorsement of policies by as many groups as possible facilitates action and increases the likelihood of success. The city corporation counsel also suggests that any public official about to launch a program involving large expenditures of money and covering a long period of time secure the support of as many groups as possible. In such cases the executive would go to groups like the Manufacturers' Association and the Chamber of Commerce to try to enlist their support. It is obvious that at this juncture these groups possess considerable influence, since they may bargain using their future support to enlicit certain changes in the program.

## Sportsmen's Groups

Let us now turn to an examination of the influence held by groups of sportsmen in this county. The general impression held by the respondents is that no such groups, with the exception of Professor Jackson's movement, are currently adopting any positive programs to fight the general pollution problem in the county. Many reflected on the late 1940s when there was a valiant attempt among a number of groups to unite behind a comprehensive antipollution program. Most agree, however, that since then there has been no serious group effort in a positive direction.

There have been a number of very successful efforts on the part of some private sportsmen to save their wetlands and hunting grounds. Ironically, one of the most successful of these efforts actually interfered with a treatment facility that was being constructed in North Syracuse. North Syracuse was developed after the war with extremely myopic haste and did not provide adequate sewage facilities. Consequently, sewers had to be constructed after the community was already in existence. The county wanted North Syracuse to comply with construction of an operation that allowed the sewage to linger and undergo oxidation in a swamp north of the city before being discharged ultimately into the Seneca River. The discharge of sewage into the swamp was begun, but it was followed quickly by a horrified outcry from a tiny group of muskrat hunters who claimed their wetlands were being destroyed. This group of muskrat hunters brought such pressure to bear that the county had to construct, at considerable expense, a pipeline that caused the sewage to bypass the swamp and discharge at a point north, where it finally entered the Seneca River. According to a disturbed official in the Health Department, there are no more than 100 people who hunt muskrats in the swamp. Another Health Department official, who has also felt the impact of small group activity, noted that solid waste disposal in Clay and Cicero was effectively blocked by groups in these two cities. An official in the Division of Drainage and Sanitation remarked that the county was to build a treatment plant in Fayetteville which conflicted with an Erie Canal Park. Disapproval was voiced at the hearing, some people were contacted, and finally the site of the plant was moved.

## DISCUSSION

What emerges rather clearly from an attempt to summarize the comparative influence of the various county institutions examined on pollution policy formation is that institutional influence varies in accordance with the character of the policy in question. The institution that is overwhelmingly agreed to be most influential on pollution policy is the county executive. However, the potential influence of this institution is usually reserved for policies having the greatest political impact, financial cost, and general community concern. A somewhat smaller but still impressive consensus sees the Division of Drainage and Sanitation as the agency most influential on the more technical and substantive aspects of pollution policy. Of course, the Division is dependent on the legislature's budgetary allotments and the administration's priorities. Nevertheless, its technical expertise gives it almost complete discretion on day-to-day operations and a very formidable role in how the larger policy decisions will be operationalized and implemented. The Board of Supervisors' (County Legislature's) influence is, for the most part, limited to the financial aspect of pollution policy. There is a consensus that the Board would rarely challenge the substantive pollution policy recommendations coming via the county executive, the Division of Drainage and Sanitation, and the Governmental Committee on Onondaga Lake, but it would be intimately concerned with financing these policies. The influence of groups is considered very relative. Most agree that the general trend of concerted action to overcome pollution is being encouraged by federal, state, and local forces and that groups will be unable to interfere with this trend. Many, however, agree that groups still have great influence on particular aspects within the overall parameters of the antipollution activities. Thus, the media, business, and industrial and sportsmen's groups might effectively get behind a specific program, although they might be unable to halt the anti-pollution trend.

# 11

## POWER, OPINION, AND POLICY LINKAGES

The intent of this study has been threefold: to examine influence relationships within one community, Syracuse, New York; to examine the state of public opinion concerning urban problems and priorities in the Syracuse community; and to examine the policy-making process in four policy areas within the community—law enforcement, social services, education, and water pollution control. It is the view here that to understand the complexity of a local political system one must investigate at least these three elements of the community: power, public opinion, and public policy-making. If one is interested in linking community power to community policy, it is necessary to identify and determine the preferences of those who have influence in the community. And if one wants to understand the dynamics of community policy, it is necessary to investigate the dynamics of not only community power relations but community preferences as well.

An additional theme underlying this survey of the Syracuse community is the necessity of examining the political process in frames of reference that are dynamic or processual. Very early in the study it was determined that static descriptions of power structures, of the composition of public opinion, or of the public policy-making arena would be inadequate to generate information concerning the dynamics of community politics. The view here of the community political system encompassed a number of interdependent elements and variables capable of change through time. Thus, the problems of conception and research design that accompany an investigation of political dynamics were accepted with the hope that a contribution has been made toward the understanding of community political systems.

## COMMUNITY AND POWER IN SYRACUSE

The fundamental question with which this part of the study was begun was whether power exists within a locality. It was desired to determine the extent to which decisions in four areas of government activity are made by local officials rather than state and federal officials. The point of departure was community power literature, particularly studies that have been made in Syracuse.

The concept of power is a crucial element in the analysis of community. The location and identity of decision-makers were considered to be fundamental to the question of whether community exists in modern America. Community is, in part, a sense, a feeling, a state of mind. It is composed of more than economic, political, or "reason"-able ties between men. It is essentially the belief that the public good exists and that the contribution of each individual is significant in attaining the public good. It is a sense of identification with the leaders who purport to represent the individual. Power signifies the connection between the existence of community and the input of the participant. If one sees that people believe they have a hand in making decisions significant to their lives, one can make a case for the existence of community.

This study does not attempt to answer this question directly, but it probes an essential aspect by asking whether local government (that government purportedly closest to man and most directly involved with his intimate concerns) has in fact any relevance to the decisions affecting his life in light of increased activity by state and federal officials. By community, then, one is indicating the belief of the residents of a locality in a shared public enterprise. This is the context within which the conclusions about influence relations and currency flows among local, state, and federal decision-makers in corresponding functional areas of government will be reviewed.

This study was begun by analyzing influence relations among these decision-makers. The 39 respondents were asked to name those government officials—local, state, and federal—with whom they believe themselves to be in influence relations and to indicate the nature of these relationships. A total of 99 other officials were mentioned. (Many of these were mentioned by more than one respondent.) The respondents and those whom they mentioned constitute a system of 138 actors, who, with the aid of a computer program, were grouped into mutual influence sets. A mutual influence set is defined as a set of actors who can influence (directly or indirectly) and be influenced by (directly or indirectly) every other decision-maker within the set. Each member of a mutual influence set, then, has either a direct or an indirect symmetrical influence relationship

with every other member of the set. The sets are, of course, disjoint.
That is to say, no actor can be a member of more than one mutual
influence set. If there were a common member, he would connect
all the members of the two sets into a single mutual influence set.

Analysis of the influence relations among these 138 government
officials yielded 63 mutual influence sets. One of these sets contains
69 actors; another, two actors; and the remaining 61 sets, only one
actor each. Since a mutual influence set contains those individuals
who share power with one another, the set was defined as an operationalization of the concept of community. It is a precise statement
of the influence relations among a group of people selected on the
basis of their having input into decisions significant to the community.
Having operationalized community as a mutual influence set, the lone
multimember set, which contains half of the government officials in
the system of 138, was examined to see what proportion of the local,
state, and federal actors in the system are in the set and what proportion are not in the set. It was possible to learn what proportion
of the members of a power community are local, state, and federal
government decision-makers. It was found that 56 percent of the
members of the set were local, 28 percent state, and 16 percent
federal decision-makers.

This finding supports those students of community power who
have defined a meaningful community to include vertical relationships
(i.e., relationships between locals and individuals outside of the
community) and the individuals with whom locals have these relationships. Nevertheless, it is noteworthy that over half the members of
this power community are locals. Local government leaders in
Onondaga County see themselves as sharing in the decision-making
process. A total of 39 locals are in this set, and 7 more exercise
influence over it. Consequently, out of a total of 58 locals in the
entire system of 138 actors, 40 of these locals are either in the
major mutual influence set or in minority control sets exercising
influence over it. This finding is significant. Locals not only share
power in the community but hold their own in relationships with other
levels of government.

In addition to investigating influence relations among the decision-makers themselves, data were gathered about the local, state,
and federal inputs to actual decisions made in the daily course of
organizational activity. In attempting to link power to policy-making,
our respondents were asked to evaluate and to rank in order of significance the influence of local, state, and federal government on
five aspects of organizational activity. These areas are funding,
establishing training programs and/or standards for professional
personnel, defining the scope of the organization, evaluating its
operational success, and formulating legal and administrative
regulations.

These data were collected because the authors agree with those
students of power who contend that direct, sensational confrontations
within the sphere of a system's activity are not the most significant
facet of that institutions's operation.  By studying the entire spectrum
of each institution's activity for a given period of time rather than a
number of decisions made at different times, the data are intended
to reflect the process of decision-making, since it is here held that the
occasions and mechanisms most likely to prove sources of policy
impacts are the regular and recurring administrative devices for
committing future production objectives, allotting basic resources,
and assigning authority to produce.  An attempt has been made to
represent the flow of interchange between local subsystems and their
extracommunity ties.  The hypothesis is that local units of government
exercise autonomous power over fewer aspects of the structure and
functioning of local public education, law enforcement, public welfare,
and water pollution control agencies/institutions than do state and
federal units of government.

The evidence does not validate this hypothesis.  It was found
that, with the exception of water pollution control, currency flow is
asymmetrical in favor of local government, because locals perceive
themselves to be primary in making these kinds of decisions.  Only
in water pollution control is the currency flow asymmetrical in
favor of the state government.  In the other three functions the state
government is somewhat secondary and the federal government
definitely tertiary.

As a part of this specific analysis of decision-making, questions
about the respondents' communication patterns with general government local officials and with state and federal officials were asked.
It was found that educators divide their extra-agency communication
between general government local and state officials, with a relatively
small proportion of it going to federal officials.  Social service
officials communicate twice as much with state officials as with
locals and a third as much with state officials.  Water pollution control officials spend the most time with local and federal officials
and the least with state officials.

The respondents were also asked how frequently they initiate
contact as compared to the frequency with which they receive messages
from general government local, state, and federal officials.  The question of who initiates communication was considered to be an operationalization of the symmetry or asymmetry of influence relations among
government officials.  When one official initiates contact more frequently than another, the first can be considered to exercise asymmetrical influence over the second.  If the actors respond to each
other an equal number of times, their influence relationship can be
considered symmetrical.  In the great majority of cases relations

were found to be symmetrical, with officials of the same level of
government as the primary initiator and the primary destination of
communications. This bore out the previous findings of the equality
of local and state officials in terms of the influence they wield.

The results of the auxiliary use of a measure less obtrusive
than the interview are, to a great extent, consistent with the interview
data. By use of the respondents' appointment calendars, their nongovernmental community, local general government, state government,
and federal government contacts were tallied and analyzed for a given
period of time. The assumptions underlying the use of these data
were the same as those on which the initiation/destination index of
the symmetry or asymmetry of influence relations was based. It was
assumed that the movement of these individuals indicates something
about the influence relationships between them. The appointment
calendar data were examined in a number of ways. A relationship
between the level of government of the person being met and the
location of the meeting (i.e., the respondent's office, the other's
office, or neutral territory) was sought. Profiles of the distribution
of visits among local others, general government locals, state officials, and federal officials were developed. The results of the
hierarchical ordering of actors as reported in Chapter 2 were compared
with the results of the analysis of appointment calendar information.
Then the results of the currency flow analysis repeated in Chapter 4
were compared with the appointment calendar information.

It was found that 56 percent of visits with general government
locals were held in local offices, 85 percent of visits with state officials
were held in state offices, and 41 percent of visits with federal officials
were held in federal offices. The rest of the visits were divided quite
evenly between the respondents' offices and neutral territory. According to this measure, influence relations between the respondents
and each of these three categories of others are asymmetrical in the
direction of the others. The correlation between the hierarchical
structuring of the actors as reported in Chapter 2 and the results of
this analysis is low.

When the appointment calendar data were analyzed in the same
way as the influence data, the results were more consistent. It had
been concluded that locals see themselves as being as influential to
decision-making in their functional areas as their counterparts at
the state and federal levels. The appointment calendar measure bore
this out, with the qualification that general government locals, at the
top level in each of the appointment calendar hierarchies, share
influence with state officials over functional area locals. The results
of the appointment calendar hierarchical structuring and the decision-
making data reported in Chapter 3 are also comparable. In Chapter
2 it was concluded that, with the exception of water pollution control

officials, all groups of respondents are either primary or share primacy with state officials. Federal officials are least significant here, as they are in the appointment calendar hierarchical structuring.

The conclusions indicate that a viable community of decision-makers does exist on the local level. At the same time, one must broaden the traditional concept of community to encompass the vertical dimension. No longer (if ever they were) are local government functions entirely the purview of local residents. Still, notwithstanding the frequent cries of obsolescence of local government, representatives of localities do believe that they have a viable role in carrying out these functions. Despite encountering significant differences from one function to another, one can conclude that, although state officials in many cases share primacy with locals, locals hold their own. The same conclusion was made with respect to currency flows among the three levels of government. In some cases locals are clearly primary in making decisions significant to the daily operation of the organizations examined. In other cases they share primacy with state officials. In no instance was it found that locals are completely overwhelmed by higher level influentials.

Some of the findings previously referred to have apparent explanations in the diverse nature of functions performed by local governments. Especially important here is the nature of relationships between officials and the particular group of citizens whom they serve and with whom they most closely identify—in a word, their constituents.

Especially noteworthy is the difference between educators and policemen on the one hand and social service officials on the other. What distinguishes these two groups is that the former have much more positive and rewarding associations with their constituents than do the latter. Policemen promote the safety of persons and property; educators promote the intellectual and social development of youth. Both groups have a personal and professional stake in believing, whatever the actual case may be, that their relationships with state and federal officials allow them to perform autonomously in creative, satisfying work. They are, therefore, willing and able to exert themselves to maximize local discretion vis-à-vis officials at higher levels of government. Beyond this, they are likely to perceive themselves to be independent actors rather than mere agents for distant power sources. So it is that the belief in, and perhaps the substance of, locally based community persists most strongly within those areas of local government in which officials are performing functions they consider important and rewarding.

Within the social service function, on the other hand, officials do not normally receive such satisfaction from their relationships with their clients. It is not surprising, therefore, that they differ from law enforcement and education officials in two respects: they do see outside forces as significant in influencing their work, and they seem quite sanguine about the situation. Indeed, social service officials expressed eagerness to have the state and federal levels take even more responsibility. (It must be acknowledged here that administrators were interviewed rather than patrolmen, teachers, or social workers. It is felt here that, although social workers might differ from the consensus of their superiors, patrolmen and teachers would be more likely to echo the views of their administrators.)

There are several policy implications in the above remarks. First, it seems clear that the judgments people make about the extent of their personal and institutional autonomy are not always related to the degree of objectively measured autonomy that seems to exist. Rather, they evaluate their relationships with others on the basis of satisfaction with their own work. The respondents seemed little concerned with the abstract question of "community control" vis-à-vis higher levels of government. They seemed quite satisfied in their capacity to use formal and informal techniques to counteract any external constraints that would otherwise be overly restrictive.

Most fundamentally, one should be reminded of the constant interplay between structure (in this case the relative influence of different levels of government) and function (the nature of policy). Although the two are analytically separable, in actual day-to-day government decision-making they are intertwined. One must be careful not to emphasize one unduly at the expense of the other.

One final observation about the relevance of the findings to policy-making is that there is little relationship between what may appear to be extracommunity controls over resources and how personnel see these controls as constraining. This fact has implications for the issue of whether to give assistance to local communities by way of categoric grants (which give aid for specific projects) or block grants (which allow recipients greater decisional latitude). Categoric grants appear to be a threat to local autonomy, since they entail more restriction on spending. But the existence of restrictions per se seems to be less important than whether such restrictions cause a deviation from professional standards within the governmental area concerned. Categoric grants may be negotiated on the basis of consensual professional standards within the governmental area concerned. Categoric grants may be negotiated on the basis of consensual professional standards. If so, they may well allow for the maximum necessary local flexibility, while providing at least a semblance of control, which makes such grants more acceptable politically than the freewheeling block grants.

The fundamental conclusion of the examination of power and influence relations among local government officials and between

local officials and state and federal government officials, then, is
that influence must be analyzed not only in terms of the objective
indicators of power but also in terms of the values, judgments, and
perceptions of local officials. And the vertical dimension of community, despite the difficulties of investigation, is well worth studying
in any thorough examination of power and decision-making in the
local political system.

## PUBLIC OPINION AND PUBLIC POLICY

The fundamental problem motivating this study of public opinion
and policy-making was to determine the extent and character of
linkages between mass opinion and public policy. The policy-making
process was described as continuous and complex, with a variety of
organizations, individuals, groups, and publics contending for influence
over policy outcomes. It is in examining the link between the public
and officials in power that one goes to the heart of a democratic
system. Despite the difficulties in designing and carrying out a study
of this nature, an attempt was made to explore the structure of public
opinion in the Syracuse community concerning public problems and
priorities, particularly in regard to four policy areas—law enforcement, social services, education, and water pollution control. Then
it was attempted to relate these preferences or perceptions to the
policy process in the four areas in Syracuse. The bulk of the information concerning these linkages deals with one specific policy area,
water pollution control, and therefore the conclusions will be based
primarily on this area.

In an earlier chapter various approaches to the analysis of
public policy formation that are suggested in political science
literature were described. None of these approaches alone could
adequately describe the linkages as found here. It was not that any
one approach failed to describe a linkage but that each approach
described only one aspect of a very complex network of relationships
that must be viewed in its entirety if one is to gain a realistic appreciation of the policy process. If, for instance, one restricted oneself
to an examination of the linkages suggested by the rational activist
mode, one would have to conclude that there is indeed very little
association between public opinion and elite response and hence not
a very democratic public policy process. Each of the various
approaches indicated some relationships, however, and when taken
in sum they provide a credible argument for the existence of a
democratic public policy process.

In the course of the research it was found that one could not
understand the public policy process adequately by focusing exclusively

on even the most important individual elements of the process. Public policy formation involves various public agencies, groups, individuals, and levels of government—each contributing differing amounts in various ways to the evolution of policy. One cannot hope to understand the overall formation of the policy by isolating any particular aspect or actor in the process. Hence, it was found that it was not appropriate to study local water pollution policy just by focusing on the county, since the state and federal governments also play critical roles in the process. The complexity of this network of interrelated actions and actors demands reflection in the network of linkages.

## The Rational Activist Model

The model that is probably responsible for eliciting the most skepticism concerning the existence of any linkage between the people and the policy process is the rational activist model. It appears rather certain that only a small minority of the population is able to gather and comprehend all relevant political information, then make rational calculations as to how they are affected individually by the variety of information they have gathered, and finally support the candidates who best reflect their preferences. If, as appears to be the case, many voters make their choice on more deterministic grounds, one may assume that these citizens are not utilizing the political process either to elect representatives who share their preferences or in other ways to work to cause policy to affect these preferences.

On the basis of the analysis, however, much of this skepticism does not seem justified. First, as has been noted in the discussion of pluralistic linkages, rational calculations are only one strand in a whole network of relationships between the people and the policy process. Second, despite the fact that only a small minority of the people appear to calculate their political choices rationally, the possibility of a larger number of people becoming aware of a policy issue makes elected politicians quite sensitive to policies that might become popular. Much of the influence of such men as Daniel Jackson is their ability to capture the imagination of the people and thereby to keep the pollution issue in the political foreground. Without any formal source of power, Jackson nevertheless is ranked as the third most influential person by the political elites interviewed. More significantly, Jackson received many more votes from elected politicians than from appointed bureaucrats. This is to be expected, since elected officials have reason to observe carefully his influence on the electorate.

The influence of the press operates in much the same manner. Since local politicians do not have opinion polls in their pockets, they must be sensitive to the political effect of newspaper editorials on public sentiment. From the evidence, however, it is clear that many editorial campaigns are not successful in directing political action.[1] One must assume, therefore, that politicians are receiving feedback from other sources, one of which is the political party.

## The Political Parties Model

The political parties model provides a variety of linkages between policy-makers and various segments of the population. One aspect in particular suggests that the party provides the citizen with an economy. Since he no longer has to calculate rationally each candidate's advantages, the citizen can consider merely which party best reflects his preferences. The linkages demonstrated by this model emerge, however, only when a party takes a definitive stand on an issue and receives the support of its strong adherents. In the case of water pollution in Onondaga County both parties are on record as favoring a major water quality improvement program. Both parties are also opposed to increased local taxes and have consequently taken the position that an improvement program must be financed primarily by extra-Onondaga County sources. The voter, therefore, has little choice.

Another type of linkage is exemplified by the party acting as an intermediary between its supporters and their elected representatives. The unique case of Onondaga County, where both city and county governments are in the hands of the same party, strengthens the position of the party as broker between the politician and the party supporter. At one point the success of industry was noted, exemplified by Solvay Process, in shaping policy through Republican Party channels. Their control of both seats of government, however, places the Republicans in a vulnerable position. The party in such a situation must keep a sensitive ear to public opinion to ensure that public dissatisfaction with city and county government does not become strong enough to manifest itself as a negative vote for the Republican administration, thereby initiating a major shift to the Democratic Party. The beginnings of such a movement may be indicated by the emerging strength of Onondaga County's third-term U.S. Congressman, Democrat James Hanley. Congressman Hanley has worked vigorously for the generation of federal funds to assist Onondaga County in its water pollution fight. If he is successful, some credibility should accrue to the contention that the local Democratic Party is more fundamentally committed to pollution control than are the Republicans.

At present, such a contention would be difficult to uphold, but Hanley's position as a conduit to Washington puts his party in a position to take credit for a funding breakthrough.

## The Group Model

Probably the largest array of ties between the public and policy processes is provided by the group model. The mere allusion to a group implies an aggregate of individuals and, hence, an aggregated body of opinion and votes. Groups, by their very nature, identify a somewhat cohesive segment of the voting population and appear more ominous to the elected politicians than an amorphous collection of individuals. The group model operated dramatically when 100 or so muskrat hunters succeeded in getting the Division of Drainage and Sanitation to build a costly pipeline to pump effluent beyond their swamp. Had it been sought, a much larger segment of the population could probably have been found to oppose this costly appropriation.

Groups may be formally organized entities, or they may be completely disorganized but still identifiable aggregates. Ethnic, professional, vocational, economic, and racial bodies of opinion fall into the latter category. The potential influence of these groups lies, obviously, in their voting strength. Few things are more fundamental to elected officials. The appointed official, however, is equally sensitive to the electoral fortunes of his legislative body; thus, he, too, must heed various pressure groups. He is likely to feel pressure from his more vulnerable elected colleagues should he try to ignore public opinion.

In chapters 5 and 8 a number of unorganized groups were identified, such as urban and suburban residents, whites and nonwhites, the young and the old, the rich and the poor, the lesser and the better educated. Also presented were findings to indicate the areas in which these unorganized groups agree and disagree. In chapters 7 and 8 the responses of political and administrative influentials to the preferences of these unorganized groups was described. In this way, the manner in which government responds to these groups and which of these groups are advantaged or disadvantaged by present policy was illustrated.

The influence on government of large industries in the county that contribute to pollution continues to be great. A large industry is a rather unique phenomenon, since it is necessarily an organized entity, often with a common interest. It employs a labor force of thousands, all sharing the interest of protecting the source of their livelihood. Thus, industries such as Allied Chemical, Crucible Steel, and Crouse-Hinds have enormous individual influence as spokesmen for the thousands they employ. Groups such as the Manufacturers'

Association, which aggregate the interests of their members, hold
even greater influence. In earlier chapters the tremendous influence
of Allied Chemical, first in blocking anti-pollution policies and
currently in supporting them was discussed. It is likely that the
only way the county will introduce tertiary treatment in the near
future is in a cooperative venture with Allied Chemical.

Partly because of their vast potential membership, unorganized
groups sometimes have greater influence on policy than do pressure
groups. The shortcoming of unorganized groups, however, is generally
an inability to use their strength in the best possible way. If a large
unorganized group can articulate its opinion clearly, it can have an
influence so great that it does not have to manipulate strategies. A
clear example is the 3-1 approval of the Pure Waters Referendum
that immediately elicited the mandate for secondary treatment
throughout the state.

It is difficult to overestimate the impact that the Pure Waters
Act had on state government officials. Probably few of them expected
such an overwhelming mandate. They were, however, quick to make
it clear to New York State voters that the state government would
respond immediately. The state advised localities that they would
not have to wait for their federal grants to construct antipollution
facilities. The state would immediately provide the locality with the
sum of the federal grant for which it was eligible, and the state would
later be reimbursed when the federal funds came. In 1966, the first
year following the referendum, four times more state and federal
funds were received by the county than in the entire preceding decade.
It is unlikely that any organized group could have elicited the response
from the state that this unexpected expression of the people did.


### The Sharing Model

An approach that elicits great skepticism as to its ability to
demonstrate linkage between the people and the policy process is the
sharing model. Indeed, if this model represented the whole claim
for a democratic policy process it would not be a very convincing
argument. It is only one facet of the pluralistic network of linkages,
however, and implications of its existence have been found quite often
in this study. For example, a number of public officials mentioned
having shared with one of the industries some contingency, such as
a job during a summer vacation. Consequently, they admitted sym-
pathy for many of the problems the companies have with pollutants.
On the other hand, many other officials noted that the last time they
passed by the lake or visited the adjacent parks they were driven
away by the odor. It seems rather clear that public officials, since

they live in the community, are at least as sensitive as the public at
large to community problems and are often much more sensitive
because of their proximity to matters of policy. It is true that this
model does not suggest any way of coping with the eventuality of the
officials' ceasing to share the view of the majority. It is similarly
true that there are many unpopular policies. In the event that an
official sponsors unpopular policies, the rational-activist model, of
course, provides the simple alternative of voting the rascal out for
someone who better represents the desires of the community.

Most criticisms of the sharing model point to studies indicating
considerable differences between political leadership and the public.
While sensitive to these differences, however, the authors note many
more similarities, which provide an important source of linkage
between political leaders and the public. For example, findings that
indicate political leadership to be more ideological than that of the
general community do not in any way indicate that these more ideological leaders do not share feelings with the people on more mundane
community needs.[2]

## The Role-Playing Model

In the role-playing model the public official sees his role most
simply as spokesman for the preferences, desires, and demands of
the public. In this study this role conception was found in elected
and appointed officals alike. In Chapter 8 this group of leaders was
described as the "democrats," those who feel the community wants
something done about pollution and who want to comply with the
wishes of the community. These officials were most impressed with
the Pure Waters Act of 1965.

Perhaps a more subtle dimension of the role-playing model
appears in what many officials sense as the momentum of the times.
The officials in this model begin typically with a long rendition of
the major problems that have had to be faced since World War II:
the housing of returning veterans, the general acceptance of the role
of government in the social welfare field, civil rights, and so on.
They continue that many of the more essential problems that have
faced the nation have been solved and that presently the United States
is in a position to turn to less ominous but still important problems,
including water pollution. Such role-playing officials feel that if one
pays close attention to activities surrounding the matter of water
pollution on the national and local levels one cannot help noticing
incremental increases in consideration given to the problem. Public
opinion is becoming more and more sensitive to the threats of un-
checked pollution, and both federal and local governments have been

responding steadily with legislation to ameliorate the situation. Hence, a crescendo is being reached as the problem becomes widely recognized. The role-playing politicians are responding more to a trend that they feel is constantly gaining momentum than to a particular demand identified in their constituencies. They see a growing consensus building around the need to do something about water pollution in much the same way as the consensus has grown around policies of social welfare and civil rights.

There are numerous ways in which the public official can articulate the desires of his constituency on matters of public policy. Many have been alluded to in the preceding models. Certainly, interest groups and political parties provide information on particular segments of the community. Even elections and campaigns provide the interested politician with exposure to and association with the people from whom at least general parameters of public opinion may be culled. The mail received by public officials contributes additional insight to the feelings of interested citizens.

The historical preoccupation of a locality with a certain policy area may influence an official in his predisposition to provide support for this policy area. The officials interviewed certainly appreciated the vision Onondaga County displayed in its early efforts to cope with water pollution, and many were quite proud of this distinction. Some officials felt that the county might have built the antipollution facilities it has today without the aid of federal and state grants. The overwhelming majority of officials, however, appreciated the critical importance of federal and state grants for the county's attack on water pollution. Nonetheless, the early activities of Onondaga County in fighting water pollution clearly influenced the public officials to be quick to take advantage of federal and state grants once they had become available. Without the evidence of the early activities officials probably would have been slower in committing the county to the many matching fund grants, awaiting more obvious indication that this policy was popular in the community.


Stress on the Model

The influence that external governments exert on the policy process of local government greatly challenges the explanatory ability of these models. The essential feature of a democratic policy process is that there be linkages between the people and the decision-makers. It was suggested that these linkages are found in a complex network wherein different people and groups have lines of communication and leverage on the political leadership. The problem posed by external governments is that their ability to provide needed funds can very often compete with and supersede the demands of public opinion in the locality.

Much of the argument concerning linkages revolves around the fact that in the last analysis the political leaders depend on the people for reelection and for support of their programs. When external governments offer up to 90 percent of the cost of greatly needed facilities, however, public opinion is often understandably overlooked. In the matter of antipollution policy in Onondaga County public opinion and the influence of external grants happened to coincide. There are many occasions, however, when external grants supersede hostile public opinion regarding policy issues in localities. Federal funds for education that require school districts to comply with desegregation formulas as a condition for eligibility clearly provide a case in point. Many financially impoverished Southern localities are reluctantly seduced to comply with desegregation because of their critical need for federal funds.

## Oligarchy or Democracy?

In the preceding discussion the ways in which various models suggest linkages between sectors of the community and elements of the policy process were analyzed. The complexity of the policy process and the numerous levels of relationship between the public and policy process indicated by different models was emphasized. It was further hypothesized that if one summed up all of the linkages indicated by the various models one would find a very convincing argument that there are democratic controls on the public policy process. There is, however, a very popular criticism of the pluralist conception of democracy. Applied to the model of pluralistic linkages, the criticism questions whether one is not indicating just how small groups are linked to the policy process. Consequently, continues the criticism, one is describing an oligarchical rather than democratic public policy process. This criticism, however, assumes erroneously that the small groups in the linkage descriptions of the various models are identical throughout. If that were the case, the various models would all be indicating linkage with the same groups to form a small elite minority and an oligarchical policy process. In the variety of models were indicated relationships with different groups in the population, however. If all the people in the different groups of the various models were combined, one would have a majority of the population, and, hence, a democratic public policy process.

## The Influence Differential

One cannot measure, however, the varying amounts of influence held by the different groups. Even within the pluralistic model of linkages it is possible for a number of groups representing a minority of the population to have more influence than groups representing a majority of the population. But this phenomenon does not mean that the policy process is undemocratic. As long as the systemic predisposition of the policy process is directed toward finding a consensus and satisfying the demands of as many of the people as possible, it is here contended that the process is essentially democratic. Clearly, in modern mass government it is impossible to take hand votes for every government policy to ensure that a majority always exists for each governmental action. If the system is geared toward the ideal of popular consent and if the possibility truly exists for the majority of the people to vote out of office the officials they feel are not representing them, then the system is democratic. Generally, if a public policy represents the demands of a minority, the majority that might oppose this policy has not articulated its views effectively. As long as there are systemic features of the policy-making process that enable the majority of people to have their demands acceded to (and the electoral process ultimately assures this), then the system is democratic.

## POLICY PRIORITIES AND PUBLIC FUNDS

Having concluded the discussion of the linkages between public opinion and public policy, one can now examine some of the findings of the public opinion poll in light of this discussion. Realizing that government can never deal with all of the problems facing it at one point in time, the authors were interested in the order of priorities that the people in the county would establish for some of the more pressing policy areas and in where water pollution would fall on this list. The results of the poll indicate that water pollution is ranked third among urban problems by all the people of the county. Breaking the county down into urban and suburban categories, it was found that water pollution still ranked a strong third among suburban residents, moving down to fifth place among urban residents. The county budget was then examined to see what expenditures were being allotted for water pollution control, assuming that the level of expenditure for a policy area is a rough indicator of the vigor with which the problem is being attacked. The model of linkages elicits the expectation that expenditures for water pollution would be large, since it is popularly considered an important problem. It was found, however, that county expenditures for water pollution control were very meager, below the outlays for policy areas lower than water pollution on the public list of priorities.

How does one explain this paradox in light of the proposition regarding linkages? First, it is not at all certain that the attention a public policy area is given by public officials is a reliable indicator of its priority among the public. Different public policies require vastly different expenditures in order to be accomplished. Second, the county budget expenditures for water pollution measures are only a small part of the money being spent on water purification. Federal and state governments provide about two-thirds of the costs of antipollution projects. Third, even if the expenditures on antipollution matters legitimately indicated that the county was not doing very much in this area, it would still not compromise the existence of a democratic policy process in the county. It is clear that there is tremendous competition for the limited funds possessed by local governments. There are already mandated programs that have to be financed. The county government may decide that more basic programs such as education and social welfare require funds that might otherwise be used for water pollution facilities. The resulting lack of expenditure for pollution matters would not then negate the existence of a democratic policy process.

The concept of democracy has traditionally been a popular subject for inquiry among political scientists. A probable reason for its popularity is the urge among students of politics to examine prevailing credos and myths about Western political systems. Many studies of democracy have been prescriptive in favor of the author's predispositions. Others have been more empirical, restricting themselves to analysis of the system as they found it. The more empirical studies have illustrated clearly that it is difficult to apply the concept of democracy to the modern mass political system. In the last analysis it remains a matter of judgment whether the variety of dramatic and subtle controls the people retain on the system are sufficient criteria to call it democratic. This study has probed a variety of linkages that are here felt to connect the people to the policy process. It is the authors' judgment that these linkages provide ample evidence of the existence of a democratic policy process.

INTRODUCTION
    1. Roscoe C. Martin et al., Decisions in Syracuse (New York: Doubleday, 1965), and Linton C. Freeman, Patterns of Local Community Leadership (Chicago: Bobbs-Merrill, 1968).
    2. Scott Greer, The Emerging City: Myth and Reality. (New York, Free Press of Glencoe, 1962), pp. 206-207.
    3. Roscoe C. Martin, "Cities," Annals, CCCLIX (May 1965), 109.
    4. John Dewey, The Public and Its Problems (Denver: Alan Swallow, 1927), p. 147.
    5. Mitchel Cohen and Dennis Hale, eds., The New Student Left (Boston: Beacon Press, 1966), pp. 9-16.
    6. Robert C. Wood, Suburbia: Its People and Their Problems (Boston: Houghton-Mifflin, 1958).

CHAPTER 1
    1. Robert S. and Helen M. Lynd, Middletown (New York: Harcourt, Brace & World, 1929), and Middletown in Transition (New York: Harcourt, Brace & World, 1937).
    2. William Lloyd Warner and Paul S. Lunt, The Social Life of a Modern Community (New Haven, Conn.: Yale University Press, 1941).
    3. Floyd Hunter, Community Power Structure (Chapel Hill: University of North Carolina Press, 1953).
    4. Willis D. Hawley and Frederick M. Wirt, eds., The Search for Community Power (Englewood Cliffs, N.J.: Prentice-Hall, 1968), p. 39.
    5. Terry N. Clark, ed., Community Structure and Decision-Making: Comparative Analysis (San Francisco, Chandler Publishing Co., 1968), p. 76.
    6. Robert Dahl, Who Governs? (New Haven, Conn.: Yale University Press, 1961).
    7. Roscoe C. Martin and Frank J. Munger, eds., Decisions in Syracuse (New York: Doubleday, 1961), p.322.
    8. Linton C. Freeman et al., Local Community Leadership, University College Publication No. 15 (Syracuse, N.Y., 1960).
    9. Martin and Munger, Decisions, p. 361.
    10. Roland L. Warren, The Community in America (Chicago: Rand McNally, 1953), p. 242.

168

11. Ibid., p. 46.

12. Ibid., p. 50.

13. Arnold Rose, The Power Structure (New York: Oxford University Press, 1967), p. 297.

14. Robert Presthus, Men at the Top (New York: Oxford University Press, 1964).

15. Freeman et al., Local Community Leadership, p. 7.

16. John Walton, "The Vertical Axis of Community Organization and the Structure of Power," in Hawley and Wirt, Search, pp. 353-66.

17. Ibid., p. 354.

18. Ibid., p. 361.

19. For examples, see Robert O. Schulze, "The Role of Economic Dominants in Community Power Structure," American Sociological Review, XXIII (February 1958), 3-9; and Roland J. Pellegrin and Charles S. Coates, "Absentee-Owned Corporations and Community Power Structure," American Journal of Sociology, LXI (March 1965), 414.

20. Walton, "Vertical Axis," p. 361.

21. Ibid., p. 362.

22. Ibid.

23. For an extended discussion of the concept of power see Rose, Power Structure pp. 43-53.

24. Hawley and Wirt, Search, pp. 2-3.

25. Karl W. Deutsch, The Nerves of Government (New York: The Free Press, 1963), p. 111.

26. Ibid., p. 117.

27. Ibid., p. 124.

28. Morton Grodzins, The American System: A New View of Government in the United States (Chicago: Rand McNally, 1966), p. 250.

29. Peter Bachrach and Norton Baratz, "Two Faces of Power," in Hawley and Wirt, Search, pp. 239-49.

30. Ibid., pp. 241-42.

31. The term is from E. E. Schattschneider, The Semi-Sovereign People (New York: Holt, Rinehart & Winston, 1960), p. 71.

32. Warren, Community, p. 167.

33. Martin and Munger, Decisions, p. 21.

34. Pellegrin and Coates, "Absentee-Owned Corporations"; Schulze, "Economic Dominants"; and John Henry Lindquist, "Businessmen in Politics: An Analysis of Political Participation in Syracuse, N. Y., 1880-1959" (unpublished Ph.D. dissertation, Syracuse University, 1961).

35. The locality-relevant function is abstracted from Warren, Community, pp. 9-11.

36. Eugene J. Webb et al., Unobtrusive Measures: Nonreactive Research in the Social Sciences (Chicago: Rand McNally, 1966).

CHAPTER 2

1. Steven J. Brams, "Measuring the Concentration of Power in Political Systems," American Political Science Review, LXII (June 1968), 461-75.

2. Ibid., p. 461.

3. Brams, "Decomp: A Computer Program for the Condensation of a Directed Graph and the Hierarchical Ordering of Its Strong Components," Behavioral Science, XIII (July, 1968). Vol. 13, 344-45.

4. Brams, "Measuring," p. 472.

5. Herbert A. Simon, "Notes on the Observation and Measurement of Political Power," in Willis D. Hawley and Frederick M. Wirt, eds., The Search for Community Power (Englewood Cliffs, N.J.: Prentice-Hall, 1968) pp. 21-25.

6. Brams, "Measuring," p. 462.

7. Ibid., p. 463.

8. Ibid., p. 464.

9. Ibid., p. 466.

10. John Walton, "The Vertical Axis of Community Organization and the Structure of Power," in Hawley and Wirt, Search, pp. 353-66.

CHAPTER 3.

1. Eugene J. Webb et al., Unobtrusive Measures: Nonreactive Research in the Social Sciences, (Chicago: Rand McNally, 1966).

2. Nicholas Pileggi, "The City Politic: Why Leary Got Out," New York Magazine, September 28, 1970, pp. 8-9.

3. See, for example, John W. Thibaut and Harold H. Kelley, The Social Psychology of Groups (New York: John Wiley and Sons, 1959), p. 125.

CHAPTER 4.

1. James Bryce, The American Commonwealth, Vol. II (London: Macmillan, 1889), p. 217.

2. This discussion relies heavily upon a number of works, most useful being Harwood Childs, Public Opinion: Nature, Formation and Role (Princeton, N.J.: D. Van Nostrand, 1965), esp. pp. 26-38.

3. John Kenneth Galbraith has noted this most forcefully in a recent book, The New Industrial State (New York: Houghton Mifflin, 1967).

4. V. O. Key suggests this strength of public opinion in his
Public Opinion and American Democracy (New York: Alfred Knopf,
1961), p. 3.

5. Robert E. Lane and David Sears, Public Opinion (Englewood
Cliffs, N.J.: Prentice-Hall, 1965), p. 1.

6. The comments are by Pascal, Montaigne, and Sir Robert
Peel.

7. Avery Leiserson, "Notes on the Theory of Opinion Formation," American Political Science Review, XLVII (1953), 171.

8. William W. and Wallace E. Lambert, Social Psychology
(Englewood Cliffs, N.J.: Prentice-Hall, 1964), p. 50.

9. Key, Public Opinion, p. 9.

10. This discussion follows somewhat that of Bernard C.
Hennessey, Public Opinion (Belmont, Cal.: Wadsworth, 1965), pp.
98-103.

11. Key, Public Opinion, p. 12.

12. Francis G. Wilson emphasizes this characteristic especially
in his A Theory of Public Opinion (Chicago: Henry Regnery, 1962),
esp. pp. 5, 82-93.

13. Key, Public Opinion, p. 14.

14. Hans Speier, "Historical Development of Public Opinion,"
American Journal of Sociology, LV (1949-50), 376.

15. Floyd H. Allport, "Toward a Science of Public Opinion,"
Public Opinion Quarterly, I (1937), 7-23.

16. Childs, Public Opinion, p. 110.

17. Hennessey discusses each of these perspectives in more
detail in Public Opinion, pp. 156-164.

18. Reo M. Christenson and Robert O. McWilliams, Voice of
the People (New York: McGraw-Hill, 1962), p. 530.

19. See Childs, Public Opinion, pp. 66-88, for an excellent
discussion of this background.

20. Ibid. p. 77.

21. Hennessey, Public Opinion, pp. 49-50.

22. Christenson and McWilliams, Voice, pp. 481, 490.

23. Hadley Cantril, Gauging Public Opinion (Princeton, N.J.:
Princeton University Press, 1944), pp. 150-71.

24. Lindsay Rogers, The Pollsters (New York: Alfred Knopf,
1949), pp. 41-42.

25. Childs offers a thorough examination of this problem
(Public Opinion, Ch. 5).

26. Ibid., p. 82.

27. Walter Lippmann, The Public Philosophy (Boston: Little,
Brown, 1955).

CHAPTER 5
1. V. O. Key, Public Opinion and American Democracy (New York: Alfred Knopf, 1961), p. 4.
2. David Hume, Essays and Treatises on Several Subjects (Dublin, 1742), Vol. I, Pt. I, IV, p. 29.
3. Harwood L. Childs, Public Opinion: Nature Formation and Role (Princeton, N.J.: D. Van Nostrand, 1965), p. 319.
4. Key, Public Opinion, p. 412.
5. Bernard C. Hennessey, Public Opinion (Belmont, Cal.: Wadsworth, 1965), p. 106.
6. Ibid., p. 107.
7. Francis G. Wilson, A Theory of Public Opinion (Chicago: Henry Regnery, 1962), p. 8.
8. Norman R. Luttbeg, ed., Public Opinion and Public Policy (Homewood, Ill.: The Dorsey Press, 1968), p. 2.
9. V. O. Key, "Public Opinion and Democratic Politics," in Luttbeg, Public Policy, p. 240.
10. Robert E. Lane, Political Life (Glencoe, Ill.: The Free Press, 1959), esp. chs. 15, 16, 17, 20, 21; Angus Campbell et al., The American Voter (New York: John Wiley, 1960), esp. chs. 6, 12, 13, 14, 15, 17; Seymour Martin Lypset, Political Man (New York: Anchor Books, 1963), chs. 6, 7, 8; Bernard R. Berelson et al., Voting (Chicago: University of Chicago Press, 1954), chs. 3, 4, 5, 6, 9; Lawrence H. Fuchs, "American Jews and the Presidential Vote," American Political Science Review, XLIX (1955), 385-401; Heinz Eulau, "Perceptions of Class and Party in Voting Behavior, 1952," American Political Science Review, XLIX (1955), 364-84; V. O. Key and Frank Munger, "Social Determinism and Electoral Decision: The Case of Indiana," in Eugene Burdick and Arthur Bradbeck, eds. American Voting Behavior (Glencoe, Ill.: The Free Press, 1959), pp. 281-99; Angus Campbell et al., The Voter Decides (Evanston, Ill.: Row, Peterson, 1954), Pt. 2.
11. Childs, Public Opinion, pp. 310-19. Among the cases included in this analysis are nuclear testing, the Kennedy steel controversy, Federal aid to education, Cuba, Medicare, and military expenditures.
12. Luttbeg, Public Policy, pp. 4-5.
13. Ibid., p. 5.
14. Ibid.
15. See Nelson W. Polsby, Community Power and Political Theory (New Haven, Conn.: Yale University Press, 1963); Robert A. Dahl, Who Governs? (New Haven, Conn.: Yale University Press, 1961); Robert Presthus, Men at the Top (New York: Oxford University Press, 1964); M. Kent Jennings, Community Influentials: The Elite of Atlanta (New York: The Free Press of Glencoe, 1964);

Robert E. Agger, Daniel Goldrich, and Bert E. Swanson, The
Rulers and the Ruled: Political Power and Impotence in American
Communities (New York:   John Wiley and Sons, 1964); and Peter
Rossi, "Community Decision Making," Administrative Science
Quarterly, I (March 1957), 419.

16. Luttbeg, Public Policy, p. 7.

17. Dahl, Who Govens?, pp. 311-25.

18. Key, Public Opinion, p. 410.

19. Alex Inkeles, Public Opinion in Soviet Russia (Cambridge,
Mass.: Harvard University Press, 1950).

20. David Easton, A Systems Analysis of Political Life (New
York:  John Wiley, 1965), p. 42.

21. Harold Lasswell, Politics:  Who Gets What, When and How
(New York:  McGraw-Hill, 1957); and Aaron Wildavsky, The Politics
of the Budgetary Process, Boston:  Little, Brown, 1964).

22. New York, State of. Executive Department. "New York
State Population Changes Since 1960." Albany, New York, December
1966.

23. See particularly Lane, Political Life; and Eugene Uyeki,
"Patterns of Voting in a Metropolitan Area," Urban Affairs
Quarterly, I (June 1966), 65-77.


CHAPTER 6

1. David Easton, A Framework for Political Analysis (Englewood Cliffs, N.J.:  Prentice Hall, 1965), p. 49.

2. Charles Lindblom, The Policy-Making Process (Englewood
Cliffs, N.J.:  Prentice Hall, 1968), p. 2.

3. Ira Sharkansky, Policy Analysis in Political Science
(Chicago:  Markham, 1970), pp. 1-19.

4. Edward V. Schneier, Policy-Making in American Government (New York:  Basic Books, 1969), p. ix.

5. Ibid., p. xi, xii

6. Ibid.

7. Easton, Framework, p. 50.

8. George A. Shipman, "Role of the Administrator:  Policy-
Making as Part of the Administering Process," in Fremont Lyden,
George Shipman, and Morton Kroll, eds., Policies, Decisions and
Organizations (New York:  Meredith, 1969), pp. 123, 134.

9. Morton Kroll, "Policy and Administration," in ibid., pp.
12-20.

10. Karl W. Deutsch, The Nerves of Government (New York:
The Free Press, 1963), p. 77.

11. Ibid., p. 111.

12. Steven J. Brams, "Measuring the Concentration of Power
in Political Systems," American Political Science Review, LXII
(June 1968), 469.

CHAPTER 7

1. U.S. Department of Commerce, Census of Governments, 1967, Compendium of Public Employment (Washington, D.C.: the Department, 1969).

2. Yehezkel Dror, Public Policy-Making Reexamined (San Francisco: Chandler, 1968), p. 95.

3. H. H. Gerth and C. W. Mills, From Max Weber: Essays in Sociology (New York: Oxford University Press, 1946), pp. 214, 232.

4. Francis E. Rourke, Bureaucracy, Politics, and Public Policy. (Boston: Little, Brown, 1969), p. 41.

5. Duane Lockard, The Politics of State and Local Government (2d ed.; New York: Macmillan, 1969) p. 395.

6. Don K. Price, Government and Science (New York: New York University Press, 1954), p. 200.

7. John C. Bollens and Henry J. Schmandt, The Metropolis (New York: Harper and Row, 1965), p. 210.

8. Lockard, Politics, p. 354.

9. Rourke, Bureaucracy, p. 2.

10. Norton Long, The Polity (Chicago: Rand NcNally, 1962), p. 53.

11. Rourke, Bureaucracy, p. 3.

12. Paul Appleby, Policy and Administration (University: University of Alabama, 1949), pp. 89-90.

13. Wallace Sayre and Herbert Kaufman, Governing New York City (New York: Russell Sage Foundation, 1960), p. 732.

14. Rourke, Bureaucracy, p. 147.

15. James Q. Wilson, Varieties of Police Behavior (Cambridge, Mass: Harvard University Press, 1968), p. 7.

16. John A. Gardiner, "Police Enforcement of Traffic Laws: A Comparative Analysis," in James Q. Wilson, ed. City Politics and Public Policy (New York: John Wiley, 1968) pp. 151-72.

17. Lockard, Politics, p. 419.

18. Wilson, Varieties, p. 230.

19. Gilbert V. Steiner, Social Insecurity: The Politics of Welfare (Chicago: Rand McNally, 1966), pp. 239-43.

20. Ibid., p. 156.

21. Harold Wilensky and Charles Lebeaux, Industrial Society and Social Welfare (New York: The Free Press, 1965), p. 268.

22. Quoted in Ibid., p. 273.

23. Martha Derthick, "Intercity Differences in Administration of the Public Assistance Program: The Case of Massachusetts," in Wilson, City Politics, pp. 243-66, esp. p. 257.

24. Keith Goldhammer et al., Issues and Problems in Contemporary Educational Administration (Eugene: University of Oregon Press, 1967, pp. 3-4.

25. Roscoe Martin, Government and the Suburban School (Syracuse, N.Y.: Syracuse University Press, 1962), p. 61.

26. Nicholas Masters, Robert Salisbury, and Thomas Eliot, State Politics and the Public Schools (New York: Alfred Knopf, 1964), pp. 265, 270.

27. Michael Kirst, ed., The Politics of Education at the Local, State and Federal Levels (Berkeley: McCutchan Publishing Co., 1970), p. 5.

CHAPTER 8

1. V. O. Key, Public Opinion and American Democracy (New York: Alfred Knopf, 1961), pp. 552-53.

2. Ibid., p. 555.

3. Key, Public Opinion.

CHAPTER 10

1. Roscoe C. Martin and Frank J. Munger, eds., Decisions in Syracuse (New York: Doubleday, 1965), pp. 318-19.

2. New York, State of. Water Pollution Control Board. "Eight Years of Water Pollution Control Progress in New York State," by A. F. Dappert, executive secretary, Albany, 1957.

3. Ibid., p. 4.

CHAPTER 11

1. Roscoe C. Martin et al., Decisions in Syracuse (New York: Doubleday, 1965), p. 321.

2. See Herbert McClosky et al., "Issue Conflict and Consensus Among Party Leaders and Followers," American Political Science Review, LIV (June 1960), 406-27.

## BOOKS

Agger, Robert E., Daniel Goldrich, and Bert E. Swanson. The Rulers and the Ruled: Political Power and Impotence in American Communities. New York: John Wiley and Sons, 1964.

Almond, Gabriel A., and Sidney Verba. The Civic Culture. Boston: Little, Brown, 1963.

Appleby, Paul. Policy and Administration. University: University of Alabama Press, 1949.

Banfield, Edward C. Political Influence. New York: The Free Press, 1961.

Bollens, John C., and Henry J. Schmandt. The Metropolis. New York: Harper and Row, 1965.

Campbell, Angus, et al. The American Voter. New York: John Wiley, 1960.

Cantril, Hadley. Gauging Public Opinion. Princeton, N.J.: Princeton University Press, 1944.

Childs, Harwood. Public Opinion: Nature, Formation and Role. Princeton, N.J.: D. Van Nostrand, 1965.

Christenson, Reo M., and Robert O. McWilliams. Voice of the People. New York: McGraw-Hill, 1962.

Clark, Terry N. Community Structure and Decision-Making: Comparative Analyses. San Francisco: Chandler, 1968.

Dahl, Robert A. A Preface to Democratic Theory. Chicago: University of Chicago Press, 1956.

_____. Who Governs? New Haven, Conn.: Yale University Press, 1961.

Deutsch, Karl W. The Nerves of Government. New York: The Free
    Press, 1963.

Dror, Yehezkel. Public Policy-Making Reexamined. San Francisco:
    Chandler, 1968.

Easton, David. A Framework for Political Analysis. Englewood
    Cliffs, N.J.: Prentice-Hall, 1965.

_____. A Systems Analysis of Political Life. New York: John
    Wiley, 1965.

Freeman, Linton C. Patterns of Local Community Leadership.
    Chicago: Bobbs-Merrill, 1968.

Gerth, H. H., and C. W. Mills. From Max Weber: Essays in Sociology.
    New York: Oxford University Press, 1946.

Goldhammer, Keith, et al. Issues and Problems in Contemporary
    Educational Administration. Eugene: University of Oregon
    Press, 1967.

Grodzins, Morton. The American System: A New View of Government
    in the United States. Chicago: Rand McNally, 1966.

Hawley, Willis D., and Frederick M. Wirt, eds. The Search for
    Community Power. Englewood Cliffs, N.J.: Prentice-Hall,
    1968.

Hennessey, Bernard C. Public Opinion. Belmont, Cal.: Wadsworth,
    1965.

Hunter, Floyd. Community Power Structure. Chapel Hill: University
    of North Carolina Press, 1953.

Jacob, Philip E., and James V. Toscano. The Integration of Political
    Communities. New York: J. B. Lippincott, 1964.

Jennings, M. Kent. Community Influentials: The Elite of Atlanta.
    New York: The Free Press of Glencoe, 1964.

Katz, Elihu, and Paul F. Lazarsfeld. Personal Influence. New York:
    The Free Press, 1955.

Key, V. O. Public Opinion and American Democracy. New York:
    Alfred Knopf, 1961.

Kirst, Michael, ed. The Politics of Education at the Local, State and Federal Levels. Berkeley: McCutchan Publishing Co., 1970.

Lane, Robert E. Political Life. Glencoe, Ill.: The Free Press, 1959.

_____, and David Sears. Public Opinion. Englewood Cliffs, N.J.: Prentice-Hall, 1965.

Lasswell, Harold. Politics: Who Gets What, When and How. New York: McGraw-Hill, 1957.

Lindblom, Charles. The Policy-Making Process. Englewood Cliffs, N.J.: Prentice-Hall, 1968.

Lippmann, Walter, The Public Philosophy. Boston: Little, Brown, 1955.

Lockard, Duane. The Politics of State and Local Government. 2d ed. New York: Macmillan, 1969.

Long, Norton. The Polity. Chicago: Rand McNally, 1962.

Luttbeg, Norman R., ed. Public Opinion and Public Policy. Homewood, Ill.: The Dorsey Press, 1968.

Lyden, Fremont, George Shipman, and Morton Kroll. Policies, Decisions and Organizations. New York: Meredith, 1969.

Lynd, Robert S. and Helen M. Middletown. New York: Harcourt, Brace & World, 1929.

_____. Middletown in Transition. New York: Harcourt, Brace & World, 1937.

Martin, Roscoe C. et al., eds. Decisions in Syracuse. New York: Doubleday, 1965.

Masters, Nicholas, Robert Salisbury, and Thomas Eliot. State Politics and the Public Schools. New York: Alfred Knopf, 1964.

Mills, C. Wright. The Power Elite. New York: Oxford University Press, 1956.

Polsby, Nelson W. Community Power and Political Theory. New Haven, Conn.: Yale University Press, 1963.

Presthus, Robert. Men at the Top. New York: Oxford University Press, 1964.

Rose, Arnold. The Power Structure. New York: Oxford University Press, 1967.

Rourke, Francis E. Bureaucracy, Politics, and Public Policy. Boston: Little, Brown, 1969.

Sayre, Wallace, and Herbert Kaufman. Governing New York City. New York: Russell Sage Foundation, 1960.

Schattschneider, E. E. The Semi-Sovereign People. New York: Holt, Rinehart & Winston, 1960.

Schneier, Edward V. Policy-Making in American Government. New York: Basic Books, 1969.

Sharkansky, Ira. Policy Analysis in Political Science. Chicago: Markham, 1970.

Stein, Maurice. The Eclipse of Community. Princeton, N.J.: Princeton University Press, 1960.

Steiner, Gilbert V. Social Insecurity: The Politics of Welfare. Chicago: Rand McNally, 1966.

Truman, David E. The Governmental Process. New York: Alfred Knopf, 1951.

Warner, William Lloyd. Yankee City. New Haven, Conn.: Yale University Press, 1963.

_____, and Paul S. Lunt. The Social Life of a Modern Community. New Haven, Conn.: Yale University Press, 1941.

Warren, Roland L. The Community in America. Chicago: Rand McNally, 1963.

_____, ed. Perspectives on the American Community. Chicago: Rand McNally, 1966.

Webb, Eugene J., et al. Unobtrusive Measures: Nonreactive Research in the Social Sciences. Chicago: Rand McNally, 1966.

Wildavsky, Aaron. The Politics of the Budgetary Process. Boston: Little, Brown, 1964.

Wilensky, Harold, and Charles Lebeaux. Industrial Society and Social Welfare. New York: The Free Press, 1965.

Wilson, Francis G. A Theory of Public Opinion. Chicago: Henry Regnery, 1962.

Wilson, James Q. Varieties of Police Behavior. Cambridge, Mass.: Harvard University Press, 1968.

_____, ed. City Politics and Public Policy. New York: John Wiley, 1968.


ARTICLES AND PERIODICALS

Allport, Floyd H. "Toward a Science of Public Opinion," Public Opinion Quarterly, I (1937), 7-23.

Bachrach, Peter, and Morton S. Baratz. "Two Faces of Power." The Search for Community Power. Edited by Willis D. Hawley and Frederick M. Wirt. Englewood Cliffs, N.J.: Prentice-Hall, 1968.

Barth, Earnest A. T., and Stuart D. Johnson. "Community Power and a Typology of Social Issues." The Search for Community Power. Edited by Willis D. Hawley and Frederick M. Wirt. Englewood Cliffs, N.J.: Prentice-Hall, 1968.

Berelson, Bernard. "Democratic Theory and Public Opinion," Public Opinion Quarterly, XVI (1952), 313-30.

Bonjean, Charles M., and David M. Olson. "Community Leadership: Directions of Research," Administrative Science Quarterly, IX (December 1964), 278-300.

Brams, Steven J. "DECOMP: A Computer Program for the Condensation of a Directed Graph and the Hierarchical Ordering of its Strong Components," Behavioral Science, XIII (July 1968), 344-45.

_____. "Measuring the Concentration of Power in Political Systems," American Political Science Review, LXII (June 1968), 461-75.

Dahl, Robert A. "The Concept of Power," Behavioral Science, II
(July 1957), 201-15.

Derthick, Martha. "Intercity Differences in Administration of the
Public Assistance Program: The Case of Massachusetts."
City Politics and Public Policy. Edited by James Q. Wilson.
New York: John Wiley, 1968.

Dorsey, John T. "A Communication Model for Administration,"
Administrative Science Quarterly, II (December 1957), 307-24.

Eulau, Heinz, and Robert Eyestone. "Policy Maps of City Councils
and Policy Outcomes: A Developmental Analysis," American
Political Science Review, LXII (1968), 124-43.

Frederickson, H. George, and Howard Magnas. "Comparing Attitudes
Toward Water Pollution in Syracuse," Water Resources Research,
IV (October 1968), 877-89.

Frederickson, H. George, "Exploring Urban Priorities," Urban Affairs
Quarterly, IV (September 1969), 31-43.

Gardiner, John A. "Police Enforcement of Traffic Laws: A Comparative Analysis." City Politics and Public Policy. Edited by James
Q. Wilson. New York: John Wiley, 1968.

Hart, Henry C. "The Dawn of a Community-Defining Federalism,"
Annals, CCCLIX (May 1965), 147-56.

Key, V. O. "Public Opinion and Democratic Politics." Public Opinion
and Public Policy. Edited by Norman R. Luttbeg. Homewood,
Ill.: The Dorsey Press, 1968.

_____, and Frank Munger. "Social Determinism and Electoral
Decision: The Case of Indiana." American Voting Behavior.
Edited by Eugene Burdick and Arthur Bradbeck. Glencoe, Ill.:
The Free Press, 1959.

Kroll, Morton. "Policy and Administration." Policies, Decisions
and Organizations. Edited by Fremont Lyden, George Shipman,
and Morton Kroll. New York: Meredith, 1969.

Leiserson, Avery. "Notes on the Theory of Opinion Formation,"
American Political Science Review, XLVII (1953), 171-77.

March, James G. "The Power of Power." The Search for Community
    Power. Edited by Willis D. Hawley and Frederick M. Wirt.
    Englewood Cliffs, N.J.: Prentice-Hall, 1968.

Polsby, Nelson. "Three Problems in the Analysis of Community
    Power," American Sociological Review, XXIV (December 1959),
    796-803.

Reiss, Albert J., Jr. "The Sociological Study of Communities."
    Perspectives on the American Community. Edited by Roland
    L. Warren. Chicago: Rand McNally, 1966.

Rossi, Peter. "Community Decision Making," Administrative Science
    Quarterly, I (March 1957), 415-43.

_____. "Power and Community Structure," Midwest Journal of
    Political Science, IV (November 1960), 390-401.

Shipman, George A. "Role of the Administrator: Policy-Making as
    Part of the Administering Process." Policies, Decisions and
    Organizations. Edited by Fremont Lyden, George Shipman,
    and Morton Kroll. New York: Meredith, 1969.

Sigel, Robert, and H. Paul Friesma. "Urban Community Leaders'
    Knowledge of Public Opinion," Western Political Quarterly,
    XVIII (1965), 881-95.

Simon, Herbert A. "Notes on the Observation and Measurement of
    Political Power." The Search for Community Power. Edited
    by Willis D. Hawley and Frederick M. Wirt. Englewood Cliffs,
    N.J.: Prentice-Hall, 1968.

Speier, Hans. "Historical Development of Public Opinion," American
    Journal of Sociology, LV (1949-50), 376-88.

Uyeki, Eugene. "Patterns of Voting in a Metropolitan Area," Urban
    Affairs Quarterly, I (June 1966), 65-77.

Walker, Jack L. "A Critique of the Elitist Theory of Democracy,"
    American Political Science Review, LX (June 1966), 285-95.

Walter, Benjamin. "Political Decision-Making in Arcadia." Urban
    Growth Dynamics. Edited by Stuart Chapin. New York: John
    Wiley, 1962.

Walton, John. "The Vertical Axis of Community Organization and the Structure of Power." The Search for Community Power. Edited by Willis D. Hawley and Frederick M. Wirt. Englewood Cliffs, N.J.: Prentice-Hall, 1968.

Wolfinger, Raymond E. "Reputation and Reality in the Study of Community Power," American Sociological Review, XXV (October 1960), 636-44.


MISCELLANEOUS

Common Council. Revised General Ordinances and Charter of the City of Syracuse, New York. Newark: Gann Codes, 1961.

Corwin, Ronald D. "School Designation in Syracuse: A Study in Community Decision Making." Unpublished Ph.D. dissertation, Syracuse University, 1968.

Frederickson, H. George. "The Federal-State Interface." Mimeo. Maxwell Graduate School, Syracuse University, November 1968.

Freeman, Linton C., et al. Local Community Leadership. University College Publication No. 5. Syracuse, N.Y., 1960.

Gargon, John. "The Politics of Water Pollution in New York State: The Development and Adoption of the 1965 Pure Waters Program." Unpublished Ph.D. dissertation, Syracuse University, 1968.

Lindquist, John H. "Businessmen in Politics: An Analysis of Political Participation in Syracuse, N.Y." Unpublished Ph.D. dissertation, Syracuse University, 1961.

Magnas, Howard L. "The Public Policy Process: Linkages Between Public Opinion and Water Pollution Policy in Onondaga County." Unpublished Master's thesis, Syracuse University, January 1969.

New York State. "New York State Population Changes since 1960." Executive Department. Albany, December 1966.

_____. State Department of Social Welfare. Public Welfare in New York State. 12th ed. Albany, March 1965.

New York State Water Resources Commission. "The Water Resources of New York State." Albany, 1966.

Onondaga Lake Scientific Council. "An Environmental Assessment of Onondaga Lake and Its Major Contributory Streams." Syracuse, N.Y.: the Council, 1966. Mimeo.

Schluter, Linda L. "A Dimension of Political Community: Local Officials Influence Relations with State and Federal Officials." Unpublished Ph.D. dissertation, Syracuse University, August 1970.

Slater, Harry G., Chairman. Citizens Welfare Study Committee. Report of The Citizens Welfare Study Committee. Onondaga County, Syracuse, N.Y., January 1967.

United States. Department of Health, Education and Welfare. "The Struggle for Clean Waters." Public Health Service Publication No. 958. Washington, D.C.: the Department of Health, Education, and Welfare, 1962.

United States. Senate Committee on Public Works. "A Study of Pollution-Water." Staff Report. June 1963.

H. GEORGE FREDERICKSON is Chairman of Graduate Programs and Professor of Public Affairs at the School of Public and Environmental Affairs, Indiana University. From 1969 to 1971 he was Associate Director of the Metropolitan Studies Program, Maxwell Graduate School, Syracuse University. Professor Frederickson is on the National Council of the American Society for Public Administration and was Chairman of the Program Committee for the 1972 Conference on Public Administration in New York City.

After serving for two years on the Board of Editors of the Public Administration Review, he became the Research and Reports Editor for that journal. Professor Frederickson is also Editor of the Sage Professional Papers in Administrative Sciences. His articles on public affairs have appeared in the Administrative Science Quarterly, International Review of Administrative Sciences, Urban Affairs Quarterly, Public Management, Water Resources Research, and Public Administration Review, and he edited the volume Politics, Public Administration and Neighborhood Control.

After receiving a master's degree in Public Administration at the University of California at Los Angeles, he took his doctorate at the University of Southern California.

LINDA SCHLUTER O'LEARY is a Research Fellow at the Educational Policy Research Center of the Syracuse University Research Corporation. She also teaches urban politics at the Continuing Education Center of Syracuse University. Dr. O'Leary completed her undergraduate studies at the State University of New York, College at Brockport and received her Ph.D. in Social Science from the Maxwell School of Syracuse University in 1970, where she specialized in metropolitan government and American political thought.

Dr. O'Leary has been involved in urban planning for the state of New York. Her responsibilities included policy planning within the areas of health, education, and employment. At present, she is the Educational Policy Research Center's Project Director for a study of education, health, and public welfare delivery systems in the Genesee/Finger Lakes Region of Upstate New York.

Dr. O'Leary published an article on American political philosophy in the spring 1969 issue of the Maxwell Review. She delivered papers at the American Political Science Association annual meeting in Chicago in 1971 and at the National Gaming Council Convention at Ann Arbor, Michigan, in October 1971.